D1127246

Betty Crocker

birthdays

Houghton Mifflin Harcourt
Boston • New York • 2014

GENERAL MILLS

Food Content and Relationship Marketing Director: Geoff Johnson

Food Content Marketing Manager: Heather Reid Liebo

Senior Editor: Grace Wells

Kitchen Manager: Ann Stuart

Recipe Development and Testing: Betty Crocker Kitchens

Photography: General Mills Photography Studios and Image Library

HOUGHTON MIFFLIN HARCOURT

Publisher: Natalie Chapman

Editorial Director: Cindy Kitchel

Executive Editor: Anne Ficklen

Senior Editor: Adam Kowit

Editorial Assistant: Molly Aronica

Managing Editor: Marina Padakis Lowry

Production Editor: Jamie Selzer

Art Director and Book Design: Tai Blanche

Interior Layout: Holly Wittenberg

Manufacturing Manager: Kimberly Kiefer

TESTED & **BettyCrocker®** KITCHENS APPROVED

The Betty Crocker Kitchens seal guarantees success in your kitchen. Every recipe has been tested in America's Most Trusted Kitchens™ to meet our high standards of reliability, easy preparation and great taste.

FIND MORE GREAT IDEAS AT
BettyCrocker.com

For information about permission to reproduce selections from this book, write to Permissions, Houghton Mifflin Harcourt Publishing Company, 215 Park Avenue South, New York, New York 10003.

www.hmhco.com

Library of Congress Cataloging-in-Publication Data:

Crocker, Betty.
  Betty Crocker birthdays.
    pages cm
  Includes index.
  ISBN 978-0-544-24580-8 (pbk.); 978-0-544-24771-0 (ebk.)
1. Birthday cakes. 2. Birthday parties. I. Title. II. Title: Birthdays.
  TX771.C69775 2014
  641.86'53—dc23
                                    2013042375

Manufactured in the United States of America

DOC 10 9 8 7 6 5 4 3 2 1

Cover photos (clockwise): Pink Almond Party Cake (page 116), Chocolate-Cherry Ice Cream Cake (page 198), Candy Bar Cookie Pops (page 166), Princess Castle Cake (page 16), Chocolate–Sour Cream Cupcakes (page 160) and Electric Guitar Cake (page 62)

Dear Friends,

Birthdays only come once a year, but we love them. From the planning to the all-important party that creates the special memories, these occasions are just the best. And what tops off a birthday party? Why the cake of course. And in this book, you'll find fun decorated and deliciously flavored cakes, cupcakes and other treats for every type of birthday, whether the special day is for a child, a teen-ager or an adult.

Want to pull out all the stops for your kid's next birthday? Look for themed parties like the Princess Party, page 14, which begins with adorable crown-shaped sandwiches and finishes with a very special Princess Castle Cake. Or celebrate a Decade Party with an elegant Tall, Dark and Stout Chocolate Layer Cake, page 41.

Then find an amazing array of cakes and cupcakes for all ages and individual birthday treats like Apple or Peach Pie Pops, pages 194 and 192, or Healthified Mini Chocolate Cheesecakes, page 188, all great ideas to make any party amazing. So start planning for that next birthday occasion—and party on!

Sincerely,
Betty Crocker

... contents ...

Birthday Parties

Hosting a birthday party can be a fun, truly memorable experience, but you will want to do some planning to make sure everything turns out just right! The perfect party does not just happen—but it is not hard to achieve. So go get your camera and with our easy ideas here, get ready to throw an amazing birthday party for a very lucky guest of honor.

Keep Invites Simple

When you are getting the invitations ready, there's no need to add more information than necessary. Include the date, time, place (address), if food or dinner will be served and who the guest of honor is. If a costume is needed, add that too.

Choose to have invitees RSVP, or you can RSVP regrets only—this will depend on the group that is invited. And of course, if it is a surprise, be sure to include that! Keep a list handy so that you can note who has responded quickly and accurately.

Hush—It's a Secret!

Surprise parties are always fun but can be a little extra work because you need to keep the party a secret! But remember, some people do not like surprises, so consider this when you are planning. If you decide on a surprise, be sure to let everyone invited know in advance so they can help you keep the secret.

Fun Favors

At the end of your party, have party favors ready for all attendees. Use the theme of the party as a guide. The favors can be as simple as candies in a small container in the colors of the party or small homemade breads in seasonal flavors.

If you are throwing a Decade Party (page 40), why not give out notecards with a fun fact printed from the year that the guest of honor was born? Or if it is the Dinosaur Party (page 24), the favors could be dinosaur puzzles from the dollar store.

Princess Doll Cake
(page 46)

Party Planning 101

A bit of simple planning ensures your guests will have fun and make fabulous memories. Don't forget to take lots of pictures!

- **Pick a theme:** This sets the tone for the party and is a good starting point when planning. First, consider the birthday person. Does he or she have hobbies, favorite food or enjoy certain places, games, etc.? If the party is for a child, think about favorite animals, toys, characters or activities. Sometimes you can play games with a child, sparking their imagination for what would be a great theme for the party and might also lead you to pick a location where the party could be held. In this book, we provide some parties that are easy to put together or can be used as inspiration.

- **Select a date, time and location:** The place can be anywhere from your home or backyard to a fancy restaurant, a favorite pizza place or even a sliding hill! Use your imagination and the seasons as a guide. You might want to have an autumn harvest birthday party at an apple orchard or a party at the beach in the hot summer. Have you ever considered a winter skiing or sliding party? If you do plan for an outdoor party, try to have an alternate location inside or use a tent in case the weather does not cooperate. Make sure that the date and time are convenient for your guest of honor before moving forward!

- **Develop a guest list and number of guests:** Consider the birthday person and who they might like to include. It's okay to ask the person if you are in doubt so that you don't miss someone who should be included.

- **Send invitations 2 to 3 weeks ahead:** They can be printed invites or, if you know attendees well, e-mail is fine too. If you send printed invites, your e-mail can be used for the RSVP, so be sure to add it. In some situations, it is okay to invite guests by phone, but a printed invite is always a good reminder for people.

- **Decide on activities:** It's always fun to have things to do that work with your theme. For instance, if you are having a Pirate Party (page 28) for a child, you might plan a treasure hunt with prizes as the treasure.

- **Plan the food:** Keep your theme in mind, remembering that the star of the party will be the cake if you're serving one. Choose the guest of honor's favorites when possible and don't be shy about asking ahead of time. Your efforts will be much appreciated! When you are planning the menu, consider foods that can be made ahead and include those too.

- **Decorate, decorate, decorate!** Following your theme, have a blast making the party area as festive as possible. Streamers, balloons, artificial or fresh flowers and banners are all fun to use. Decorate the table around your theme too. For instance, if you are having the Princess Party (page 14), set the table with pretty pink doilies and delicate flowers. For some parties, the food can become part of the decoration— the Princess Castle Cake (page 16) is a good example. It could be the centerpiece of your table—so use your imagination.

- **Greet the guests as they arrive:** Whether they are children, teenagers or adults, make them feel comfortable and show each guest to the designated party area.

Make It an Ice Cream Party!

Create some glamour and fun for a birthday party with a variety of ice cream, frozen yogurt and sherbet flavors plus tasty toppings. The selection and display can be as festive as you like, showcasing a variety of colors and textures. Start with the ideas we have here as inspiration for your party—then use your imagination to create your own ideas. It's a fun way to celebrate and you won't miss the cake!

1 **Blueberry Pomegranate Bonanza:** Top blueberry ice cream with scoops of fresh blueberries. Drizzle with bottled pomegranate juice and garnish with pomegranate seeds.

2 **Cake 'n Ice Cream:** Cut frozen pound cake into 1-inch squares. Serve in dessert dishes with chocolate ice cream and drizzle with raspberry or strawberry ice cream topping. Garnish with fresh fruit.

3 **Caramel Brownie Sundaes:** Cut chocolate brownies into small squares. Layer in dessert dishes with caramel or caramel swirl ice cream and drizzle with chocolate sauce.

4 **Caramel Pecan Topper:** Drizzle caramel ice cream topping over vanilla ice cream or frozen yogurt. Sprinkle with pecans and chopped dark chocolate candy.

5 **Fresh Berry Topper:** In a medium bowl, mix 1 cup each fresh blueberries, raspberries and boysenberries. Sprinkle with 2 tablespoons orange juice; let stand about 1 hour. Serve over vanilla ice cream or lemon sherbet.

6 **Melon Mania:** Top orange sherbet with cantaloupe, honeydew and watermelon balls. Drizzle with fresh lime juice and garnish with lime peel.

7 **Peach and Granola Parfaits:** Layer peach ice cream with granola and thinly sliced peaches in dessert dishes.

8 **Peanuts and Ice Cream:** Top chocolate ice cream with coarsely chopped honey-roasted peanuts. Add small scoops of peanut butter and fudge sauce.

9 **Strawberries 'n Cream Topper:** Top strawberry ice cream with sliced fresh strawberries and sliced bananas. Top with whipped cream.

· MENU ·

TREASURE MAP PIZZA

FRUIT SHIP

PIRATE CAKE

ROOT BEER

SNACKS: MERMAID BAIT
PEG LEGS x CANNON BALLS
PIRATE'S BOOTY x FISH

themed parties

IF YOUR LITTLE GIRL WEARS A TIARA around the house and has been known to wish on every star, it may be time to throw her a majestic princess party complete with an impressive magical castle cake. Whether she has a favorite fairy-tale princess or has been asking to wear something pink and sparkly, you can be sure that she and her maidens will love an afternoon of enchantment. So go ahead and stage a medieval court of elegance, complete with a royal table, fabulous food and girlish fun fit for a princess!

Create a pretty table with a pink tablecloth, doilies, colorful confetti and child-size plates. Flowers in small vases add that final touch. Pick up paper tiaras for the little princesses at the paper or craft store. Or assemble a craft table for the girls to make their own tiaras. Include craft paper, markers, small costume jewels, feathers and glue.

For the food, start with our magic potion of Sparkling Raspberry Lemonade. Poured into small bottles adorned with special labels makes it party-perfect and ready to be served in pretty paper cups. Then add PB&J sandwiches cut into themed shapes (we like crowns) and fruit wands made by threading cutout fruit shapes on colored or plain skewers. Make the Jeweled Princess Chex Mix to use for party favors—it's simply white chocolate–covered Chex cereal with a royal sprinkling of edible glitter—yum!

Then make a spectacular cake for dessert. The Princess Castle Cake is perfect for the little ladies, or you can make the Princess Doll Cake on page 46 if you prefer. Either one of the cakes is perfect for the occasion, and your little princesses are sure to have the time of their lives.

Finally, make a menu board by adding an old frame to a chalkboard from the craft store.

Royal
MENU
~~~~~~~~~~~~

⋆ Crown PB & J

⋆ Fruit Wands ⋆

⋆ Princess
CHEX MIX

⋆ SPARKLING ⋆
Raspberry Lemonade

⋆ Tale ⋆
PRINCESS CAKE

Princess Castle Cake

PREP TIME: 40 Minutes • START TO FINISH: 4 Hours 25 Minutes • 30 servings

2   boxes yellow cake mix with pudding

2   cups water

1   cup vegetable oil

6   eggs

3½ containers fluffy white whipped ready-to-spread frosting

Red food color

Tray or cardboard (18×18 inches), covered with wrapping paper and plastic wrap, or foil

5   ice cream cones with pointed ends

Pink colored sugar

5   candy stars

28 sugar cubes

4   pink gum balls

5   pink sugar wafer cookies

1   tube (4.25 oz) white decorating icing

1 Heat oven to 350°F (325°F for dark or nonstick pans). Grease bottoms and sides of 4 (8-inch) square pans with shortening or spray with cooking spray. In large bowl, beat 1 cake mix, 1 cup of the water, ½ cup of the oil and 3 eggs using electric mixer on low speed 30 seconds, then on medium speed 2 minutes, scraping bowl occasionally. Divide batter between 2 of the pans.

2 Bake 2 pans at a time for 23 to 29 minutes (26 to 34 minutes for dark or nonstick pans) or until toothpick inserted in center comes out clean. Cool 10 minutes; remove from pans to cooling racks. Cool completely, about 30 minutes. Repeat with remaining cake mix, water, oil and eggs. Freeze cakes 45 minutes before cutting to reduce crumbs.

3 Spoon frosting into large bowl. Stir in enough food color until desired pink color; set aside. Using serrated knife, cut off domed top from each cake so they will be flat when stacked. On tray, place 1 cake, cut side down; spread ⅓ cup frosting over top. Add second cake, cut side down; spread top with ⅓ cup frosting. Add third cake, cut side down; do not frost.

4 Cut fourth cake into quarters. Spread small amount of frosting on center of cake, about the size of a cake quarter. Place 1 quarter, cut side down, on top of frosting. Spread top of stacked cake quarter with 1 tablespoon frosting. Place second quarter on top of first quarter; spread top with 1 tablespoon frosting. Add third quarter; do not frost. Cut fourth quarter into quarters to create four 2-inch squares. Spread a small dollop of frosting on the top center of the second tier of cakes. Place one 2-inch piece on the center; spread top with frosting. Top with one more 2-inch piece. (Discard remaining 2 pieces.) Spread thin layer of frosting over layered cake to seal in crumbs. Freeze cake 30 to 60 minutes.

5 Frost cones with frosting; roll in pink sugar. Frost cake with remaining frosting. Place 1 upside-down cone on each corner of the first cake layer and 1 on top cake layer for center steeple. Top each cone with candy star.

6 Place sugar cubes around edges of the first and second layers. Top each of the 4 corner sugar cubes with a gum ball. Attach 2 cookies on one side of first layer to create doors. Cut 2 additional cookies to desired size for windows; place each cookie on opposite sides of doors. Cut remaining cookie in half; place 1 half in center of second layer to create accent window. Pipe on window panes and door knobs with white icing. Store loosely covered.

1 Serving (Cake and Frosting Only): Calories 360; Total Fat 17g (Saturated Fat 4.5g, Trans Fat 2.5g); Cholesterol 40mg; Sodium 260mg; Total Carbohydrate 49g (Dietary Fiber 0g); Protein 2g **Exchanges:** ½ Starch, 3 Other Carbohydrate, 3½ Fat **Carbohydrate Choices:** 3

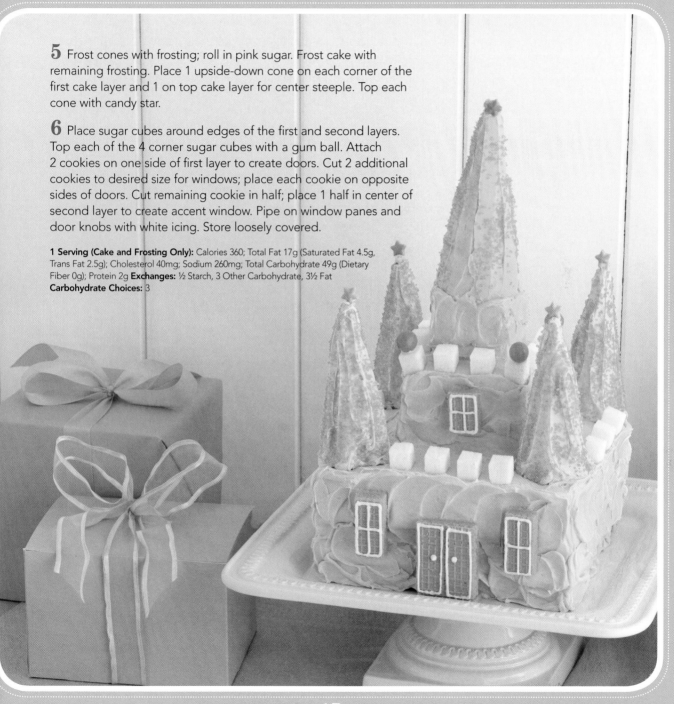

Sparkling Raspberry Lemonade

PREP TIME: 10 Minutes • **START TO FINISH: 3 Hours 10 Minutes** • **24 servings (about 1 cup each)**

2 packages (10 oz each) frozen raspberries in syrup, thawed

2 cans (12 oz each) frozen pink lemonade concentrate, thawed

2 cans (11½ oz each) frozen raspberry juice cocktail concentrate, thawed

12 cups water

4 cans (12 oz each) lemon-lime carbonated beverage

1 lemon, thinly sliced

1 Carefully spoon raspberries with syrup into 2 ice cube trays. Add enough water to just cover raspberries. Freeze 3 hours or until firm.

2 In very large plastic or glass pitcher, mix lemonade concentrate, raspberry juice concentrate and water. Refrigerate until serving time.

3 Just before serving, stir carbonated beverage into lemonade mixture. Place ice cubes in glasses; pour lemonade mixture over ice. Garnish with lemon slices.

1 Serving: Calories 150; Total Fat 0g (Saturated Fat 0g, Trans Fat 0g); Cholesterol 0mg; Sodium 20mg; Total Carbohydrate 37g (Dietary Fiber 1g); Protein 0g **Exchanges:** 2½ Other Carbohydrate **Carbohydrate Choices:** 2½

Jeweled Princess Chex Mix

PREP TIME: 10 Minutes • START TO FINISH: 30 Minutes • 24 servings (½ cup each)

- 8 cups Rice Chex® or Corn Chex® cereal
- 2 bags (12 oz each) white vanilla baking chips (4 cups)
- 2 tablespoons pink edible glitter

1 Line cookie sheet with foil or waxed paper. Place cereal in large bowl.

2 In medium microwavable bowl, microwave baking chips uncovered on High about 2 minutes, stirring every 30 seconds, until chips can be stirred smooth. Pour over cereal in bowl; toss to evenly coat.

3 Spread mixture in single layer on cookie sheet. Immediately sprinkle with edible glitter. Let stand until set, about 20 minutes. Gently break up mixture. Store in airtight container at room temperature.

1 Serving: Calories 190; Total Fat 8g (Saturated Fat 7g, Trans Fat 0g); Cholesterol 0mg; Sodium 125mg; Total Carbohydrate 27g (Dietary Fiber 0g); Protein 2g **Exchanges:** ½ Starch, 1½ Other Carbohydrate, 1½ Fat **Carbohydrate Choices:** 2

sweet tip

If you can't find edible glitter, use ¼ cup pink coarse sugar instead.

Cheerios First Birthday Party

SO YOUR LITTLE ONE IS TURNING 1—what an exciting time! And what better way to celebrate than with a party at home Cheerios-style. Gather family and friends to celebrate with an inspired first birthday that will make great memories for all.

When it comes to 1-year olds, Cheerios are always a winner, so include creative centerpiece bowls filled with a variety of Cheerios. Be sure to make some kid-friendly party foods like Mini Corn Dogs on a Stick (just make sure to remove the toothpicks before serving the little ones!). We think the perfect dessert for this special occasion is the First Birthday Smash Cake.

A smash cake for a special birthday is a fun trend that is very popular. The birthday baby or child can simply "smash" the cake into pieces and then eat it. Sometimes the cakes are small but can be regular size too. Our version is extra moist with ripe bananas, cream cheese and yogurt, plus it is covered with beloved Cheerios—this is a smash-worthy cake little ones will love!

First Birthday Smash Cake

PREP TIME: **40 Minutes** • START TO FINISH: **1 Hour 15 Minutes** • **24 servings**

1 box yellow cake mix with pudding

1 cup mashed very ripe bananas (2 medium)

½ cup vegetable oil

¼ cup water

3 eggs

1 package (8 oz) cream cheese, softened

1 container (6 oz) French vanilla low-fat yogurt

Golden yellow gel or paste food color

½ cup Cheerios® cereal

sweet tip

If you are short on time, substitute canned fluffy white frosting in place of the frosting in this recipe. Add food color to get the desired color.

*If you don't have a 6-inch round cake pan, use an 8-inch round cake pan instead. Fill pan with 2½ cups batter and bake 25 to 30 minutes. Use the remaining batter to make 15 cupcakes. Make a paper template for a 6-inch circle. Place the template on the 8-inch cake and use it to cut out a 6-inch round cake.

1 Heat oven to 350°F (325°F for dark or nonstick pans). Grease bottom only of 1 (6-inch) round cake pan* with shortening or spray with cooking spray; place paper baking cup in each of 16 regular-size muffin cups.

2 In large bowl, beat cake mix, bananas, oil, water and eggs with electric mixer on low speed 30 seconds. Beat on medium speed 2 minutes, scraping bowl occasionally until smooth. Place 1¾ cups batter in 6-inch round pan. Spoon remaining batter into 16 lined muffin cups.

3 Bake round cake 35 to 40 minutes and cupcakes for 18 to 23 minutes or until toothpick inserted in cake comes out clean. Cool 10 minutes; remove from pans to cooling rack. Cool completely, about 30 minutes.

4 In small bowl, beat cream cheese and yogurt with electric mixer on medium speed until creamy and smooth. Stir in food color until mixture is desired color.

5 To frost and decorate cake, slice 6-inch round cake horizontally to remove rounded top. Place cake cut side down on plate. Frost top and sides with cream cheese frosting. Place 2 rows of cereal around the bottom edge of side of cake. Place 1 row of cereal around top edge of cake. In top center of cake, arrange cereal to form the number one.

6 Use remaining frosting to frost cupcakes. Top with cereal to decorate, if desired. Store cake and cupcakes loosely covered in refrigerator.

1 Serving: Calories 170; Total Fat 9g (Saturated Fat 3g, Trans Fat 0g); Cholesterol 35mg; Sodium 190mg; Total Carbohydrate 20g (Dietary Fiber 0g); Protein 2g **Exchanges:** ½ Starch, 1 Other Carbohydrate, 1½ Fat **Carbohydrate Choices:** 1

Mini Corn Dogs on a Stick

PREP TIME: 30 Minutes • **START TO FINISH: 45 Minutes** • **40 servings (1 corn dog each)**

40   wooden toothpicks

1   package (16 oz) cocktail-size hot dogs (about 40 pieces)

1   can (12 oz) refrigerated flaky biscuits (10 biscuits)

1   egg, beaten

1   tablespoon milk

½   cup cornmeal

1   tablespoon sugar

¾   cup ketchup

¾   cup yellow mustard

1 Heat oven to 400°F. Grease cookie sheet with shortening or spray with cooking spray.

2 Insert toothpick into narrow end of each hot dog. Separate dough into 10 biscuits; carefully divide each biscuit horizontally into 4 rounds. Wrap sides and top of each hot dog with dough round, pinching edges to seal.

3 In pie plate, mix egg and milk. On a plate, mix cornmeal and sugar. Roll each wrapped hot dog in egg mixture, then roll lightly in cornmeal mixture. Place seam side down on cookie sheet.

4 Bake 10 to 12 minutes or until tops are light golden brown and bottoms are golden brown. Remove from cookie sheet with spatula. Serve with ketchup and mustard.

1 Serving: Calories 70; Total Fat 4g (Saturated Fat 1.5g, Trans Fat 0g); Cholesterol 10mg; Sodium 310mg; Total Carbohydrate 7g (Dietary Fiber 0g); Protein 2g **Exchanges:** ½ Starch, ½ Fat **Carbohydrate Choices:** ½

sweet tip

Add a kick to these mini corn dogs by stirring ⅛ teaspoon ground red pepper (cayenne) into the cornmeal mixture.

Dinosaur Party

FOR A BIRTHDAY PARTY OF PREHISTORIC PROPORTIONS, think dinosaurs. A Jurassic-era bash is fun to create and kids will love it! Start with a menu board (we used a fun metal board with crayons from the craft store), and gather Jurassic decorations from your backyard, like ferns and stones.

Make Stegosaurus Sandwiches with slices of ham and cheese—and cut them into dinosaur shapes. The Dino Eggs are a fun fruit salad of green grapes, kiwifruit and honeydew melon balls. For the Veggies and Bog Dip, stir green food color into ranch dressing, sprinkle with chives and serve with colorful veggies. To make the green Prehistoric Punch, stir 2 cups sugar with 2 cups water in large pitcher or punch bowl until the sugar is dissolved. Stir in 2 packages lime-flavored unsweetened soft drink mix (0.13 ounce each), 1 can pineapple juice (46 ounces) and 4¼ cups ginger ale.

And be sure to make the adorable Rex the Dinosaur Cake. It's easy to make with cake mix, frosting and chocolate candies—and the budding archaeologists will love it!

Rex the Dinosaur Cake

PREP TIME: 30 Minutes • **START TO FINISH:** 4 Hours • 15 servings

1 box devil's food cake mix with pudding

1 cup water

Vegetable oil and eggs called for on cake mix box

Tray or cardboard (18×15 inches), covered with wrapping paper and plastic wrap, or foil

2 containers vanilla creamy ready-to-spread frosting

Green gel food color

19 milk chocolate candy drops or pieces, unwrapped

Assorted round chocolate candies (candy-coated chocolate candies, miniature candy-coated chocolate baking bits, coating wafers, chocolate chips)

White decorating icing (from 4.25-oz tube)

1 Heat oven to 350°F (325°F for dark or nonstick pans). Spray bottoms and sides of 2 (8- or 9-inch) round cake pans with baking spray with flour.

2 Make and bake cake mix as directed on box, using water, oil and eggs. Cool 10 minutes. Remove from pans to cooling racks. Cool completely, about 1 hour. Refrigerate or freeze 30 to 60 minutes for easier handling.

3 For body, cut 1-inch slice from edge of one cake. From cut edge, cut out small inverted U-shape piece. Place body on tray. From remaining cake, cut head and tail. Arrange head and tail pieces next to body.

4 Spoon frosting into large bowl. Stir in enough food color until desired green color. Spread thin layer of frosting over cake pieces to seal in crumbs. Refrigerate or freeze cake 30 to 60 minutes to set frosting.

5 Frost cake pieces with remaining frosting. Use milk chocolate candies for spikes along back of dinosaur. Decorate body with assorted candies. Use 2 candy-coated chocolate candies for eyes and white decorating icing to make centers of eyes and teeth. Store loosely covered.

1 Serving (Cake and Frosting Only): Calories 430; Total Fat 18g (Saturated Fat 4g, Trans Fat 3.5g); Cholesterol 40mg; Sodium 370mg; Total Carbohydrate 63g (Dietary Fiber 0g); Protein 2g **Exchanges:** 1 Starch, 3 Other Carbohydrate, 3½ Fat **Carbohydrate Choices:** 4

sweet tips

Use a variety of candies to make your dinosaur come alive.

Create a patch of grass for your dino by coloring coconut with green food color.

Bronto Bones

PREP TIME: **2 Hours 45 Minutes** • START TO FINISH: **3 Hours 15 Minutes** • **4 dozen cookies**

1 pouch (1 lb 1.5 oz) sugar cookie mix

⅓ cup butter, softened

2 tablespoons all-purpose flour

1 egg

24 pretzel rods, broken in half

3 cups white vanilla baking chips (18 oz)

1 Heat oven to 350°F. In medium bowl, stir cookie mix, butter, flour and egg until soft dough forms. Refrigerate dough to chill slightly, about 30 minutes.

2 Roll dough into 96 half-tablespoon-size balls. Press and roll 1 dough ball around both ends of each pretzel to form bone shape; place 1 inch apart on ungreased cookie sheets. Repeat with remaining dough and pretzels.

3 Bake 6 to 8 minutes or until edges are light golden brown. Cool completely on cooling rack, about 15 minutes.

4 In small microwavable bowl, microwave baking chips uncovered on High in 30-second increments until melted when stirred. Dip each cookie into coating. Place on cooling rack until set, about 15 minutes.

1 Cookie: Calories 140; Total Fat 5g (Saturated Fat 3g, Trans Fat 0g); Cholesterol 10mg; Sodium 160mg; Total Carbohydrate 20g (Dietary Fiber 0g); Protein 2g **Exchanges:** ½ Starch, 1 Other Carbohydrate, 1 Fat **Carbohydrate Choices:** 1

sweet tip

Use vanilla-flavored candy coating (almond bark) for the white vanilla baking chips, if desired.

DINO BITES

STEGOSAURUS SANDWICHES

VEGGIES & BOG DIP

BRONTO BONES

PREHISTORIC PUNCH

dino eggs

CAKE

Pirate Party

AHOY, MATEYS! Swashbuckling good times await young pirates brave enough to join a high-sea adventure. The search for riches and gold starts with a treasure map pizza and ends with treats for all.

For the Treasure Map Pizza, make a refrigerated pizza crust as the package directs and top with your favorite pizza sauce and shredded mozzarella cheese. Add a trail of sliced black olives, green pepper and pretzel trees and a red bell pepper pirate ship. To make the Watermelon Pirate Ship, just carefully carve the sides and add a set of do-it-yourself paper sails. Fill it with a variety of fruit. Under-the-Sea Cookie Pops make great take-home party favors. And don't forget the one-eyed Pirate Cake!

Have more fun with the theme: Festive stickers turn root beer bottles into Jolly Roger pop—a pirate's drink of choice! Finish the party table with a menu written on brown paper and framed.

· MENU ·
TREASURE
MAP PIZZA
FRUIT SHIP
PIRATE CAKE
ROOT
BEER
SNACKS: MERMAID BAIT
PEG LEGS × CANNON BALLS
PIRATE'S BOOTY × FISH

Pirate Cake

PREP TIME: 30 Minutes • **START TO FINISH:** 3 Hours 45 Minutes • **12 servings**

1   box any flavor cake mix with pudding

      Water, vegetable oil and eggs or egg whites called for on cake mix box

      Tray or cardboard (15×12 inches), covered with wrapping paper and plastic wrap, or foil

1   cup chocolate creamy ready-to-spread frosting (from 1-lb container)

1½   containers vanilla creamy ready-to-spread frosting

1   chocolate-covered mint patty

1   large marshmallow, cut in half

1   blue gum ball or candy-coated chocolate candy

1   yellow ring-shaped hard candy

1   roll strawberry or other red chewy fruit snack in 3-foot rolls (from 4.5-oz box)

1   black licorice rope

      Square-shaped candy-coated gum

      Chocolate candy sprinkles

1 Heat oven to 350°F (325°F for dark or nonstick pans). Grease bottoms and sides of 1 (8-inch) and 1 (9-inch) round cake pan with shortening or spray with cooking spray.

2 Make and bake cake mix as directed on box for round cake pans, using water, oil and eggs. Cool 10 minutes. Remove from pans to cooling racks. Cool completely, about 30 minutes. For easier handling, refrigerate or freeze cake 30 to 60 minutes or until firm.

3 Use serrated knife to cut 9-inch cake in half and cut hat as shown in diagram. Remaining half of 9-inch cake will form body of pirate. Cut 8-inch cake as directed in diagram. On tray, arrange cake pieces. Cut ears and nose from small pieces of cake; attach to cake with small amount of frosting.

4 In small bowl, stir 2 teaspoons chocolate frosting into 1⅓ cups of the vanilla frosting. Frost cake with thin layer of frosting to seal in crumbs, using tinted frosting on head, ears and nose, chocolate frosting on hat, and white frosting on shirt of pirate. Refrigerate or freeze 30 to 60 minutes to set frosting.

5 Frost entire cake, using the same frostings. Add mint patty for eye patch, marshmallow slice and gum ball for eye, and ring-shaped candy for earring. Cut fruit snack into shapes for shirt stripes, mouth and strap for eye patch; place on cake. Cut licorice to fit hat. Add gum for teeth and chocolate candy sprinkles for whiskers. Store loosely covered.

1 Serving (Cake and Frosting Only): Calories 520; Total Fat 22g (Saturated Fat 5g, Trans Fat 4.5g); Cholesterol 50mg; Sodium 420mg; Total Carbohydrate 79g (Dietary Fiber 0g); Protein 2g **Exchanges:** 5½ Other Carbohydrate, 4½ Fat **Carbohydrate Choices:** 5

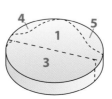
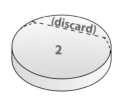
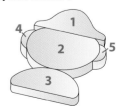

Under-the-Sea Cookie Pops

PREP TIME: 1 Hour • START TO FINISH: 3 Hours 5 Minutes • 18 cookie pops

1 pouch (1 lb 1.5 oz) peanut butter cookie mix

2 tablespoons all-purpose flour

3 tablespoons vegetable oil

1 tablespoon water

1 egg

18 paper lollipop sticks

   Cookie icing in desired colors

1 tube (0.68 oz) black decorating gel

   Orange, blue and green sanding sugars

   Candy eyes, if desired

sweet tip

Make these pops with sugar cookie mix as an alternative to the peanut butter mix.

1 In medium bowl, stir cookie mix, flour, oil, water and egg until soft dough forms. Shape dough into a ball; flatten slightly. Wrap dough in plastic wrap; refrigerate 1 hour or until firm.

2 Heat oven to 350°F. On lightly floured surface, roll dough to ¼-inch thickness with rolling pin. Cut with 3½-inch fish- and starfish-shaped cookie cutters. On ungreased cookie sheets, place cutouts 2 inches apart. Insert 1 lollipop stick halfway into center of each cookie.

3 Bake 9 to 11 minutes or until edges are lightly browned. Cool 5 minutes. Remove from cookie sheets to cooling racks. Cool completely. Decorate cookies with icing, gel and sugars. Attach candy eyes. Let stand until set.

1 Cookie Pop: Calories 150; Total Fat 7g (Saturated Fat 1.5g, Trans Fat 0g); Cholesterol 10mg; Sodium 140mg; Total Carbohydrate 20g (Dietary Fiber 0g); Protein 2g **Exchanges:** ½ Starch, 1 Other Carbohydrate, 1½ Fat **Carbohydrate Choices:** 1

Superhero Party

HAPPY BIRTH DAY!

CALLING ALL SUPERHEROES AND DEFENDERS OF PLANET EARTH! This party is action-packed and could be a page right out of one of your favorite comic books.

Crime fighters know how to work up a hunger—it's part of the job. So when it comes to feeding them, nothing short of hero sandwiches will do. Throw in some melon fruit pops, veggie roasted potato chips, an incredible hero cake plus colorful soda to wash it all down, and you've got a meal of epic proportions.

The sandwiches are super easy and can be stacked with each superhero's favorite ingredients. To make the Fruit Power Pops, start by cutting each fruit into 2-inch slices—we used watermelon, cantaloupe and honeydew. Then, use a biscuit cutter or drinking glass to create circles and a smaller shaped cutter to cut out the stars in the middle of each circle. Pop out the small stars and swap with a different melon flavor for fun color combinations. Skewer each pop through both the circle and the center with a wooden candy stick.

For the soda, look for fun colors of pop—we used vibrant-colored Mexican sodas and added labels and bold straws.

Be sure to check out the dollar store or your favorite craft place for placemat paper, containers and other party decorations. We found bright and colorful candy super suckers at the dollar store—it's fun to send each crime fighter home with a special "crime-fighting" label!

Superhero Cake

PREP TIME: 45 Minutes • **START TO FINISH: 4 Hours** • **12 servings**

1 box yellow cake mix
with pudding

Water, vegetable oil and
eggs called for on cake
mix box

Tray or cardboard (18×15
inches), covered with
wrapping paper and plastic
wrap, or foil

2 containers creamy white
or fluffy white whipped
ready-to-spread frosting

Blue food color

Yellow food color

Red food color

2 brown candy-coated
chocolate candies

1 tube (0.68 oz) black
decorating gel

2 rolls chewy fruit snack,
any flavor (from 5-oz box)

1 Heat oven to 350°F (325°F for dark or nonstick pan). Grease bottom only of 13×9-inch pan with shortening or spray with cooking spray.

2 Make and bake cake mix as directed on box for 13×9-inch pan, using water, oil and eggs. Cool 10 minutes. Run knife around side of pan to loosen cake; remove from pan to cooling rack. Cool completely, about 1 hour. For easier handling, refrigerate or freeze 30 minutes to 1 hour or until firm.

3 Use serrated knife to cut cake into head, arms and body (as shown in diagram). Place cake on serving plate or foil-covered tray.

4 In medium bowl, mix 1 container frosting and blue food color. Divide second container of frosting among 3 small bowls; add yellow to 1 bowl and red to 1 bowl; leave third bowl white. Spread thin layer of blue frosting on body and arms to seal in crumbs. Spread thin layer of white frosting on head. Refrigerate or freeze 30 minutes to 1 hour or until firm.

5 Spread remaining white frosting on head. With ½ cup of the blue frosting, create mask on face. Spread remaining blue frosting to cover body and arms. Generously spread yellow frosting on top of head for hair and at bottom of cake for belt. In center of body, spread red frosting in oval shape. Create lightning bolt with yellow frosting on red oval. Add candies on mask for eyes. Use decorating gel to pipe nose and mouth, and to outline oval, belt and belt buckle. Crumple fruit snacks; place next to body to look like cape.

1 Serving: Calories 550 (Calories from Fat 210); Total Fat 23g (Saturated Fat 5g, Trans Fat 4.5g); Cholesterol 45mg; Sodium 440mg; Total Carbohydrate 83g (Dietary Fiber 0g); Protein 2g **Exchanges:** 1 Starch, 4½ Other Carbohydrate, 4½ Fat **Carbohydrate Choices:** 5½

sweet tip

To turn superhero boy into superhero girl, use red string licorice to create long hair on the cake.

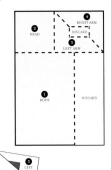

Surprise Birthday Party for All Ages

PLAN YOUR SURPRISE PARTY FOR SOMEONE who will truly enjoy all of your efforts! It's easy to throw a surprise party for kids, but putting one together for adults can require a little more finesse and sneaky planning. But whether kids or grown-ups, be sure the invitations clearly state that it is a surprise, then make a fake appointment with the guest of honor so the person does not get double-booked.

For the food, consider platters of meats, cheeses, and breads or buns for sandwiches—include all of the extras like lettuce, tomato slices, cucumber slices and mayonnaise or other sauces. For dessert, Surprise Cupcake Cones, a throwback to parties you had as a kid, make for a wonderful nostalgic treat at the end of the night.

Surprise!

Surprise Cupcake Cones

PREP TIME: 40 Minutes • **START TO FINISH: 1 Hour 25 Minutes** • **18 cupcake cones**

1 box yellow cake mix with pudding

Water, vegetable oil and eggs called for on cake mix box

1 cup candy-coated chocolate candies

18 flat-bottom ice cream cones

3 containers strawberry whipped ready-to-spread frosting

¼ cup candy sprinkles

sweet tips

If the strawberry frosting is not available, tint vanilla creamy ready-to-spread frosting a light pink with red food color.

If you have only one pan and a recipe calls for more cupcakes than your pan will make, cover and refrigerate the rest of the batter while baking the first batch. Cool the pan about 15 minutes, then bake the rest of the batter, adding 1 to 2 minutes to the bake time.

1 Heat oven to 350°F (or 325°F for dark or nonstick pans). Place paper baking cup in each of 18 regular-size muffin cups; place mini paper baking cup in each of 18 mini muffin cups.

2 Make cake batter as directed on box, using water, oil and eggs. Spoon batter evenly into regular and mini muffin cups.

3 Bake mini cupcakes 10 to 14 minutes, regular cupcakes 15 to 20 minutes (18 to 24 minutes for dark or nonstick pans), or until toothpick inserted in center comes out clean. Remove from pans to cooling racks. Cool completely, about 30 minutes.

4 If ice cream cone holder is unavailable, make a holder for the cones by tightly covering the tops of 2 empty square or rectangular pans (at least 2 to 2½ inches deep) with heavy-duty foil. With sharp knife, cut 18 "stars" in foil, 3 inches apart, by making slits about 1 inch long.

5 Place about 2 teaspoons candies in each ice cream cone. Remove paper cups from cupcakes. For each cone, frost top of 1 regular cupcake with frosting; turn upside down onto a cone. Frost bottom (now the top) of cupcake. Place 1 mini cupcake upside down on frosted regular cupcake; frost side of regular cupcake and entire mini cupcake completely (it's easiest to frost from the cone toward the top). Sprinkle or decorate with candy sprinkles. Push cone through foil opening in cone holder; the foil will keep it upright. Store loosely covered.

1 Cupcake Cone: Calories 490; Total Fat 23g (Saturated Fat 7g, Trans Fat 3.5g); Cholesterol 35mg; Sodium 250mg; Total Carbohydrate 68g (Dietary Fiber 0g); Protein 2g **Exchanges:** ½ Starch, 4 Other Carbohydrate, 4½ Fat **Carbohydrate Choices:** 4½

Half Birthday Party

WHO SAYS YOU CAN ONLY CELEBRATE YOUR BIRTHDAY ONCE A YEAR? A half birthday party can be a pleasant surprise for someone that you want to honor, or it can just be an excuse to have some fun! It can be very casual and low key—it's all about the people and having a great time.

Food for a party like this can be anything that you and your family or friends like—pizza or sandwiches are perfect. But remember the theme— set half of the table, serve "half pizzas" and "half sandwiches" and if you are using paper plates—well, you get the idea!

Make dessert colorful and fun by making our Rainbow Layer Cake—it's easy to do and is a perfect half addition to the party table! So go ahead and throw a really fun half-birthday party for someone special in your life. Happy Halfsies!

Rainbow Layer Cake

PREP TIME: **30 Minutes** • START TO FINISH: **2 Hours** • **12 servings**

CAKE

2	boxes vanilla cake mix with pudding
2	cups water
1	cup vegetable oil
6	eggs
2	packages (2.7 oz each) classic gel food colors

FROSTING

1	cup shortening
1	cup butter, softened
1	bag (2 lb) powdered sugar
2	teaspoons vanilla
3	to 4 tablespoons milk

1 Serving: Calories 1070; Total Fat 56g (Saturated Fat 19g, Trans Fat 1g); Cholesterol 135mg; Sodium 690mg; Total Carbohydrate 136g (Dietary Fiber 0g); Protein 5g **Exchanges:** 1½ Starch, 7½ Other Carbohydrate, 11 Fat **Carbohydrate Choices:** 9

sweet tips

If you only have 2 (8-inch) cake pans, bake the cakes in three batches instead.

For even better protection against cakes sticking to the pans, line pans with cooking parchment paper cut to fit the pan.

1 Heat oven to 350°F. Spray 3 (8-inch) round cake pans with cooking spray.

2 In large bowl, beat cake mix, water, oil and eggs with electric mixer on low speed 30 seconds, then on medium speed 2 minutes, scraping bowl occasionally. Divide batter evenly among 6 small bowls, about 1⅓ cups each.

3 Using food colors, tint batter in 1 bowl blue, 1 bowl red, 1 bowl green, 1 bowl yellow, 1 bowl orange (using red and yellow) and 1 bowl purple (using blue and red).

4 Refrigerate 3 colors of batter until ready to bake. Pour remaining 3 colors of batter into cake pans.

5 Bake 18 to 20 minutes or until cake springs back when touched lightly in center and begins to pull away from side of pan. Cool 10 minutes. Remove from pans to cooling racks. Cool completely.

6 Wash cake pans. Bake and cool remaining 3 cake layers as directed.

7 In large bowl, beat shortening and butter with electric mixer on medium speed until light yellow. On low speed, gradually beat in powdered sugar. Beat in vanilla. Add milk, 1 tablespoon at a time, beating until frosting is smooth. Beat on high speed until light and fluffy.

8 Trim rounded tops off cakes to level, if needed. On serving plate, place purple cake layer. Spread with frosting to within ¼ inch of edge. Repeat with blue, green, yellow, orange and red cake layers. Spread light coat of frosting on top and side of cake to seal in crumbs, then frost with remaining frosting.

9 For the half birthday cake, just make the whole cake as directed. Then, cut the cake in half for serving. Serve one half, and when you need seconds, bring out the other half!

Decade Party

FORGET THOSE KIDS TURNING 20 OR 30. Major birthdays—40, 50, 60 and up—are milestone events. These birthdays are an achievement, marking the completion of a decade, with all of its successes and experiences. Plus there is always the promise of more to come! But most of all, milestone birthdays are a wonderful reason to celebrate in a big way—so let's have a party!

Invite friends for a special dinner party with a table set for memories. Serve favorite cocktails or a favorite wine. Then choose an easy, elegant meal that is a favorite of the birthday person. Dessert is always the best part at an occasion like this, and big birthdays deserve something over-the-top decadent. Tall, Dark and Stout Chocolate Layer Cake is perfect for a special occasion—it's chocolaty rich with caramel and whipped cream. Serve slices garnished with extra whipped cream for added wow!

Tall, Dark and Stout Chocolate Layer Cake

PREP TIME: 40 Minutes • START TO FINISH: 3 Hours 30 Minutes • 16 servings

CAKE

1 box devil's food cake mix with pudding

1¼ cups stout beer

⅓ cup vegetable oil

3 eggs

FROSTING

12 oz semisweet baking chocolate, finely chopped

1½ cups whipping cream

½ cup butter

FILLING AND GARNISH

6 tablespoons caramel topping

Chocolate-covered caramels with sea salt, if desired

1 Heat oven to 350°F (325°F for dark or nonstick pans). Grease bottoms only of 3 (9- or 8-inch) round cake pans.

2 Make cake batter as directed on box, using beer, oil and eggs. Pour about 1½ cups batter into each pan.

3 Bake 18 to 22 minutes or until toothpick inserted in center comes out clean. Cool 10 minutes before removing from pans. Cool completely.

4 Meanwhile, for frosting, place chocolate in medium bowl. In 2-quart saucepan, heat cream and butter just to boiling over medium heat. Pour cream mixture over chocolate; stir with whisk until melted and smooth. Cover; refrigerate 1 hour. Stir; refrigerate about 1 hour to 1 hour 30 minutes longer or until spreading consistency.

5 Place 1 cake layer on serving plate. Frost top of layer with 1 cup of the frosting. Drizzle with 3 tablespoons caramel topping. Top with another cake layer, 1 cup of the frosting and remaining 3 tablespoons caramel topping. Top with remaining cake layer and frosting. Garnish with chunks of chocolate-covered caramels with sea salt.

1 Serving: Calories 420; Total Fat 26g (Saturated Fat 13g, Trans Fat 0.5g); Cholesterol 80mg; Sodium 320mg; Total Carbohydrate 42g (Dietary Fiber 2g); Protein 4g **Exchanges:** 1 Starch, 2 Other Carbohydrate, 5 Fat **Carbohydrate Choices:** 3

cakes just for kids

Party Ice Cream Cake

PREP TIME: 10 Minutes • **START TO FINISH: 5 Hours 45 Minutes** • **16 servings**

1 box party rainbow chip cake mix with pudding

Water, vegetable oil and eggs called for on cake mix box

1 quart frozen yogurt (any flavor), slightly softened

Candy decorations, fresh fruit or whipped cream, as desired

1 Heat oven to 350°F (325°F for dark or nonstick pan).

2 Make, bake and cool cake as directed on box for 13×9-inch pan, using water, oil and eggs.

3 Spread frozen yogurt over top of cake. Immediately cover; freeze at least 4 hours or until firm.

4 Just before serving, top each serving as desired. Cover; freeze any remaining cake.

1 Serving: Calories 240; Total Fat 10g (Saturated Fat 2.5g, Trans Fat 0g); Cholesterol 45mg; Sodium 250mg; Total Carbohydrate 34g (Dietary Fiber 0g); Protein 4g **Exchanges:** 2 Other Carbohydrate, ½ Milk, 1 Fat **Carbohydrate Choices:** 2

sweet tip

To make the frozen cake easier to cut, remove it from the freezer 20 to 30 minutes before serving.

Princess Doll Cake

PREP TIME: 40 Minutes • **START TO FINISH: 3 Hours 40 Minutes** • **30 servings**

2 boxes yellow cake mix with pudding

Water, vegetable oil and eggs called for on cake mix boxes

3 containers fluffy white whipped ready-to-spread frosting

Neon pink food color

1 fashion doll (11½ inches tall)

Pink decorating sugar

Edible pink pearls

1 Heat oven to 325°F. Grease 1½-quart ovenproof bowl (8 inches across top) and 3 (8-inch) round cake pans with shortening; coat with flour (do not use cooking spray). In large bowl, make cake batter as directed on boxes, using water, oil and eggs. (Both boxes of cake mix can be made at one time; do not make more than 2 boxes, and do not increase beating time.) Pour 3¼ cups batter into 1½-quart bowl, and divide remaining batter among 3 pans, using slightly less than 2 cups per pan.

2 Bake cake pans 23 to 30 minutes and bowl 47 to 53 minutes or until toothpick inserted in center comes out clean. Cool 10 minutes. Remove cakes from pans and bowl to cooling racks. Cool completely, about 1 hour. Place cakes in freezer 45 minutes before cutting to reduce crumbs. Cut off rounded tops of cakes. Cut bowl cake in half horizontally. Cut 1¾-inch diameter hole in center of all 5 cake layers.

3 Spoon frosting into large bowl. Stir in food color until desired pink color. Place one 8-inch cake on serving plate; spread ⅓ cup frosting over top. Top with second 8-inch cake; spread with ⅓ cup frosting. Repeat with third layer; top with larger bowl cake layer, cut side up. Spread with small amount of frosting. Top with rounded bowl cake layer, cut side down. Trim side of cake if necessary to make a tapered "skirt."

4 Spread thin layer of frosting over side and top of layered cake to seal in crumbs. Freeze cake 30 to 45 minutes to set frosting.

5 Spread frosting over cake as desired. Wrap hair and lower half of doll with plastic wrap. Insert doll into center of cake. Frost body of doll. Decorate with sprinkles and candy pearls as desired. Unwrap hair. Fashion doll is not edible; do not eat. Store cake loosely covered.

1 Serving (Cake and Frosting Only): Calories 370; Total Fat 16g (Saturated Fat 3.5g, Trans Fat 2.5g); Cholesterol 40mg; Sodium 310mg; Total Carbohydrate 56g (Dietary Fiber 0g); Protein 2g **Exchanges:** ½ Starch, 3 Other Carbohydrate, 3 Fat **Carbohydrate Choices:** 4

Ladybug Cake

PREP TIME: 35 Minutes • **START TO FINISH: 2 Hours 40 Minutes** • **12 servings**

1 box yellow or white cake mix with pudding

Water, vegetable oil and eggs or egg whites called for on cake mix box

1 container vanilla whipped ready-to-spread frosting

Black paste food color

Red paste food color

3 tablespoons red sugar

1 large marshmallow, cut in half

Chocolate or black licorice string, cut into 2-inch pieces

Chocolate-covered candies

1 Heat oven to 350°F. Generously grease 2-quart round heatproof bowl with shortening; lightly flour.

2 Make cake mix as directed on box, using water, oil and eggs or egg whites. Pour batter into bowl.

3 Bake 50 to 55 minutes or until toothpick inserted in center comes out clean. Cool 10 minutes. Run knife around side of bowl to loosen cake; remove from bowl to cooling rack. Cool completely, about 1 hour.

4 On serving plate, place cake, rounded side up, trimming bottom if needed. In small bowl, mix ½ cup of the frosting and the black food color until blended. Mix remaining frosting and red food color until blended. Spread red frosting on two-thirds of cake; sprinkle with red sugar.

5 Spread black frosting on remaining one-third of cake for head. Place remaining black frosting in decorating bag fitted with small round tip. Pipe wings and add chocolate-covered candies to make dots on sugared portion of cake.

6 Add marshmallow pieces for eyes; pipe pupils with black frosting and attach chocolate-covered candies to frosting. Pipe red frosting for mouth. Insert licorice pieces into cake for antennae. Store cake loosely covered.

1 Serving: Calories 380; Total Fat 18g (Saturated Fat 4.5g, Trans Fat 2g); Cholesterol 45mg; Sodium 310mg; Total Carbohydrate 53g (Dietary Fiber 0g); Protein 2g **Exchanges:** ½ Starch, 3 Other Carbohydrate, 3½ Fat **Carbohydrate Choices:** 3½

Train Cake

PREP TIME: **45 Minutes** • START TO FINISH: **3 Hours 30 Minutes** • **15 servings**

1 box yellow or devil's food cake mix with pudding

1 cup water

½ cup vegetable oil

3 eggs

2 containers vanilla creamy ready-to-spread frosting

Red, yellow, blue and green paste or gel food colors

1 container chocolate creamy ready-to-spread frosting

Assorted colors licorice twists and gumdrops

2 chocolate-covered caramel candies

2 creme-filled chocolate sandwich cookies, crumbled

Gummy or jellied candy rings

Assorted candies (gumdrops, jelly beans, candy corn, etc.)

1 Heat oven to 350°F (325°F for dark or nonstick pans). Grease bottoms only of 2 (8×4- or 9×5-inch) loaf pans with shortening or spray with cooking spray. In large bowl, beat cake mix, water, oil and eggs with electric mixer on low speed 30 seconds, then on medium speed 2 minutes. Pour into pans.

2 Bake yellow cake 28 to 36 minutes (devil's food cake 31 to 39 minutes) or until toothpick inserted in center comes out clean. Cool 10 minutes. Run knife around sides of pans to loosen cakes; remove from pans to cooling racks. Cool completely, about 1 hour. For easier handling, refrigerate or freeze cake 30 to 60 minutes or until firm.

3 Meanwhile, divide vanilla frosting evenly among 4 small bowls; tint 1 bowl frosting red, 1 bowl yellow, 1 bowl blue and 1 bowl green with food colors. Spoon ½ cup chocolate frosting into resealable food-storage plastic bag; set aside.

4 Using serrated knife, cut rounded top off each cake to level surface; place each cake cut side down on cutting board. Refer to diagram to assemble train. Cut first cake to make engine, do not cut all the way through piece #1 when removing piece #2. Place piece #2 on top of piece #1 with frosting between pieces. Cut second cake into 4 pieces for cars. Spread thin layer of chocolate frosting over top and sides of engine to seal in crumbs. For each of the car cakes, spread thin layer of red, yellow, blue or green frosting over top and sides to seal in crumbs. Refrigerate or freeze cakes 30 to 60 minutes or until frosting is set.

5 Snip off small corner of bag with chocolate frosting. Pipe train tracks onto serving tray. Frost engine cake with remaining chocolate frosting. Frost box cars with remaining colored frosting. Using large spatula, transfer cakes to serving tray. Cut pieces of licorice twist; place on front of engine, slanting outward, for the cowcatcher.

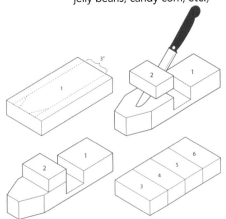

Use licorice twist to add "trim" to engine. Add gumdrops for engine "face" and chocolate candies for smoke stack. Top back of engine with crumbled cookies. Add gummy candy rings for wheels. Cut pieces of licorice twist to add "trim" to each of the cars. Add gummy candy rings for wheels. Top each car with assorted candies. Store cake loosely covered.

1 Serving (Cake and Frosting Only): Calories 420; Total Fat 17g (Saturated Fat 4g, Trans Fat 4g); Cholesterol 35mg; Sodium 330mg; Total Carbohydrate 64g (Dietary Fiber 0g); Protein 1g **Exchanges:** ½ Starch, 4 Other Carbohydrate, 3½ Fat **Carbohydrate Choices:** 4

Piano Cake

PREP TIME: 40 Minutes • **START TO FINISH: 3 Hours 30 Minutes** • **12 servings**

1   box cake mix with pudding (any flavor)*

Water, vegetable oil and eggs or egg whites called for on cake mix box

Tray or cardboard (15×12 inches), covered with wrapping paper and plastic wrap, or foil

2   bars (3.5 oz each) white chocolate candy

1   bar (1.55 oz) milk chocolate candy

1½   containers chocolate creamy ready-to-spread frosting

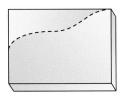

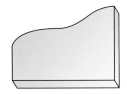

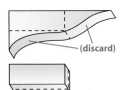

1 Heat oven to 350°F (325°F for dark or nonstick pan).

2 Make cake as directed on box for 13×9-inch pan, using water, oil and eggs or egg whites. Cool 10 minutes. Run knife around sides of pan to loosen cake; remove from pan to cooling rack. Cool completely, about 1 hour. For easier handling, refrigerate or freeze cake 30 to 60 minutes or until firm.

3 Use serrated knife to cut cake as shown in diagram (for piano bench, cut 4½×1½-inch piece; cut horizontally in half to make bench lower than piano, if desired). Place cake on tray. Place about 2 tablespoons frosting in small resealable food-storage plastic bag; seal bag and set aside. Frost cake with thin layer of frosting to set crumbs. Refrigerate or freeze 30 to 60 minutes to set frosting. Frost entire cake.

4 Cut 1 bar white chocolate into 1¾×½-inch strips. From remaining bar, cut 2½×1½-inch piece for music. Cut milk chocolate into 1×⅜-inch pieces. Place white and milk chocolate pieces on cake for piano keys. Cut off tiny corner of bag with frosting; pipe frosting notes on white chocolate "music." Place above keys. Store cake loosely covered.

1 Serving: Calories 530; Total Fat 25g (Saturated Fat 9g, Trans Fat 3.5g); Cholesterol 50mg; Sodium 420mg; Total Carbohydrate 73g (Dietary Fiber 0g); Protein 3g **Exchanges:** 1 Starch, 4 Other Carbohydrate, 5 Fat **Carbohydrate Choices:** 5

*For all chocolate and devil's food cake mixes, use only 1 cup of the water.

sweet tip

To make it easier to cut the chocolate bars, have them at room temperature. Heat a sharp knife in hot water and dry it before cutting the chocolate.

First Birthday Lion Cake

PREP TIME: 40 Minutes • **START TO FINISH: 1 Hour 55 Minutes** • **8 servings**

1 box yellow cake mix with pudding

1 cup mashed very ripe bananas (2 medium)

½ cup vegetable oil

¼ cup water

3 eggs

1 package (8 oz) cream cheese, softened

1 container (6 oz) French vanilla low-fat yogurt

Golden yellow gel or paste food color

Orange gel or paste food color

¾ cup Cheerios cereal

6 pretzel sticks

2 brown candy-coated peanut butter pieces or chocolate candies

Brown decorating gel

*If you don't have a 6-inch round cake pan, use an 8-inch round cake pan instead. Fill pan with 2½ cups batter; bake 25 to 30 minutes. Use remaining batter to make 15 cupcakes. Make a paper template for a 6-inch circle. Place template on 8-inch cake and use it to cut out a 6-inch round cake.

1 Heat oven to 350°F (325°F for dark or nonstick pans). Grease bottom only of 1 (6-inch) round cake pan* with shortening or spray with cooking spray; place paper baking cup in each of 16 regular-size muffin cups.

2 In large bowl, beat cake mix, bananas, oil, water and eggs with electric mixer on low speed. Beat on medium speed 2 minutes, scraping bowl occasionally, until smooth. Place 1¾ cups batter in 6-inch round pan. Divide remaining batter evenly among muffin cups.

3 Bake round cake 35 to 40 minutes and cupcakes 18 to 23 minutes or until toothpick inserted in center comes out clean. Cool 10 minutes. Remove from pans to cooling rack. Cool completely, about 30 minutes.

4 In small bowl, beat cream cheese and yogurt on medium speed with electric mixer until creamy and smooth. Stir in yellow food color until mixture is desired color. Place 3 tablespoons of yellow frosting in small bowl; add orange food color to get desired color.

5 To frost and decorate cake, slice 6-inch round cake horizontally to remove rounded top. Place cake cut side down on plate. Use yellow frosting to frost top and side of cake. Use orange frosting to make muzzle of lion. Place cereal around top edge of cake to form the lion's mane. Add brown candy pieces for eyes. Insert pretzel sticks into cake near muzzle for whiskers. Use brown decorating gel to make mouth, nose and whisker spots on the lion face. Use remaining frosting to frost cupcakes. If desired, use cereal to decorate cupcakes. Store cake and cupcakes in refrigerator.

1 Serving: Calories 520; Total Fat 28g (Saturated Fat 10g, Trans Fat 0g); Cholesterol 100mg; Sodium 540mg; Total Carbohydrate 60g (Dietary Fiber 1g); Protein 7g **Exchanges:** 1½ Starch, 2½ Other Carbohydrate, 5½ Fat **Carbohydrate Choices:** 4

Trix Cereal Crunch Cake

PREP TIME: 20 Minutes • **START TO FINISH: 1 Hour 20 Minutes** • **12 servings**

1 box white cake mix with pudding

Water, vegetable oil and egg whites called for on cake mix box

Yellow, red, neon green and neon blue liquid food colors

2 teaspoons grated orange peel

2 teaspoons grated lime peel

1 container fluffy white whipped ready-to-spread frosting

½ cup Trix® cereal, coarsely crushed

1 Heat oven to 350°F (325°F for dark or nonstick pans). Grease bottoms only of 2 (8- or 9-inch) round cake pans with shortening or spray with cooking spray.

2 Make cake batter as directed on box, using water, oil and egg whites. Divide batter evenly between 2 bowls (about 2 cups each). To batter in 1 bowl, add 25 drops yellow food color and 4 drops red food color; mix well. Stir in orange peel. Pour into 1 cake pan. To second bowl, add 25 drops neon green food color and 2 drops neon blue food color; mix well. Stir in lime peel. Pour into second cake pan.

3 Bake and cool cakes as directed on box for round cake pans.

4 On serving plate, place green cake layer, rounded side down. Spread with ⅓ cup of the frosting. Top with orange cake layer, rounded side up. Frost side and top of cake with remaining frosting. Sprinkle cereal on top of cake.

1 Serving: Calories 330; Total Fat 14g (Saturated Fat 3.5g, Trans Fat 2g); Cholesterol 0mg; Sodium 320mg; Total Carbohydrate 50g (Dietary Fiber 0g); Protein 2g **Exchanges:** 1 Starch, 2½ Other Carbohydrate, 2½ Fat **Carbohydrate Choices:** 3

sweet tip

Neon food color gives the brightest color, but you can substitute regular food color if you don't have neon.

Electric Guitar Cake

PREP TIME: 1 Hour 30 Minutes • **START TO FINISH:** 4 Hours 30 Minutes • **12 servings**

CAKE

1 box yellow or devil's food cake mix with pudding

1 cup water

½ cup vegetable oil

3 eggs

Tray or cardboard (19×11 inches), covered with wrapping paper and plastic wrap, or foil

FROSTING AND DECORATIONS

1¼ cups chocolate creamy ready-to-spread frosting

Black food color

2¾ cups vanilla creamy ready-to-spread frosting (from two 1-lb containers)

Desired food color for guitar

4 pieces black licorice coil, uncoiled, or string licorice

4 small chewy fruit candies in desired color

6 chewy fruit-flavored gumdrops (not sugar coated) in desired color

2 candy-coated tropical fruit-flavored candies in desired color

1 Serving (Cake and Frosting Only):
Calories 460; Total Fat 19g (Saturated Fat 4.5g, Trans Fat 4g); Cholesterol 40mg; Sodium 380mg; Total Carbohydrate 68g (Dietary Fiber 0g); Protein 2g **Exchanges:** 1 Starch, 3½ Other Carbohydrate, 3½ Fat **Carbohydrate Choices:** 4½

1 Heat oven to 350°F (325°F for dark or nonstick pan). Grease or spray bottom and sides of 13×9-inch pan. In large bowl, beat cake mix, water, oil and eggs with electric mixer on low speed 30 seconds, then on medium speed 2 minutes. Pour into pan.

2 Bake as directed on box for 13×9-inch pan. Cool 10 minutes. Remove from pan to cooling rack. Cool completely, about 1 hour. For easier handling, refrigerate or freeze cake 30 to 60 minutes or until firm.

3 Meanwhile, in medium bowl, mix chocolate frosting and black food color to make black frosting. In small bowl, mix ⅓ cup of the vanilla frosting and black food color to make gray frosting. Place gray frosting and ⅔ cup white vanilla frosting in separate resealable freezer plastic bags; seal bags. Cut small corner off each bag. In another medium bowl, mix remaining vanilla frosting and desired food color to make guitar color.

4 Using serrated knife, cut rounded top off cake to level surface; place cake cut side down on work surface. Cut cake as shown in diagram. Place cake pieces on tray as directed in diagram, attaching to tray with small amount of frosting. Spread thin layer of guitar frosting over top and sides of guitar body to seal in crumbs. Spread thin layer of black frosting over top and sides of guitar neck and headstock. Refrigerate or freeze cake 30 to 60 minutes to set frosting.

5 Frost entire cake with same colors. If desired, place remaining black frosting in resealable freezer plastic bag and cut small corner off bag to pipe frosting. To extend guitar neck 1 to 2 inches onto body of guitar, pipe and fill in neck with black frosting. With white vanilla frosting, pipe and fill in contrasting design on body of guitar. On white design, pipe black rectangle about 1 inch from end of neck to create pickup. With gray frosting, pipe on frets, bridge and any additional accents as desired. For strings, add black licorice. Add small fruit candies at ends of strings. For tuning pegs, add gumdrops. For buttons on body, add tropical fruit candies. Store cake loosely covered.

NECK

BODY | BODY

BODY

NECK

Balloon Fun Cake

PREP TIME: 15 Minutes • **START TO FINISH:** 2 Hours 25 Minutes • **16 servings**

2⅓ cups all-purpose flour

1⅔ cups sugar

¾ cup butter, softened

⅔ cup unsweetened baking cocoa

1½ cups water

3½ teaspoons baking powder

1 teaspoon salt

3 eggs

1 container fluffy white whipped ready-to-spread frosting

5 coconut-covered marshmallow bonbon cookies

6 pieces string licorice

1 Heat oven to 350°F. Grease bottom and sides of 13×9-inch pan with shortening; lightly flour.

2 In large bowl, beat all ingredients except frosting, cookies and licorice with electric mixer on low speed 30 seconds, scraping bowl constantly. Beat on high speed 3 minutes, scraping bowl occasionally. Pour into pan.

3 Bake 35 to 40 minutes or until toothpick inserted in center comes out clean. Cool 10 minutes. Remove from pan to cooling rack. Cool completely, about 1 hour 30 minutes.

4 Spread frosting on top and sides of cake. Decorate with cookies and licorice to look like balloons on strings.

1 Serving: Calories 410; Total Fat 16g (Saturated Fat 8g, Trans Fat 1.5g); Cholesterol 60mg; Sodium 410mg; Total Carbohydrate 63g (Dietary Fiber 1g); Protein 4g **Exchanges:** 1½ Starch, 2½ Other Carbohydrate, 3 Fat **Carbohydrate Choices:** 4

Tie-Dye Poke Cake

PREP TIME: 35 Minutes • **START TO FINISH: 2 Hours 30 Minutes** • **15 servings**

1   box white cake mix
    with pudding

    Water, vegetable oil and
    egg whites called for on
    cake mix box

1   cup boiling water

3   tablespoons each
    strawberry-flavored,
    lime-flavored and berry
    blue–flavored gelatin
    (from 4-serving-size boxes)

1   container vanilla whipped
    ready-to-spread frosting

4   tubes (0.68 oz each)
    decorating gel (pink, green,
    orange and blue)

1   box (17.6 oz) neon fondant

1 Heat oven to 350°F (325°F for dark or nonstick pan). Spray bottom only of 13×9-inch pan with baking spray with flour.

2 Make and bake cake mix as directed on box for 13×9-inch pan, using water, oil and egg whites. Cool in pan on cooling rack 20 minutes.

3 Meanwhile, in 3 separate bowls, pour ⅓ cup of the boiling water over each flavored gelatin; stir until gelatin is dissolved. Poke warm cake every inch with wooden skewer halfway into cake, twisting skewer back and forth. Pour each color gelatin randomly over cake, allowing gelatin to fill in holes. Cool completely, about 1 hour.

4 Frost cake. With decorating gels, draw vertical lines ¼ inch apart on frosting, alternating colors. Pull fine-tip paintbrush in straight line across all colors. Repeat, working back and forth from one side of cake to the other to create a tie-dye effect.

5 With rolling pin, roll out fondant to ⅛-inch thickness. Cut fondant into rounds and flower shapes. Insert toothpicks halfway into cutouts; decorate cake slices as desired.

1 Serving: Calories 420; Total Fat 12g (Saturated Fat 3g, Trans Fat 1.5g); Cholesterol 0mg; Sodium 270mg; Total Carbohydrate 76g (Dietary Fiber 0g); Protein 2g **Exchanges:** ½ Starch, 4½ Other Carbohydrate, 2½ Fat **Carbohydrate Choices:** 5

Pony Cake

PREP TIME: 1 Hour 30 Minutes • **START TO FINISH: 4 Hours** • **12 servings**

1 box yellow or devil's food cake mix with pudding

1 cup water

½ cup vegetable oil

3 eggs

1 container vanilla creamy ready-to-spread frosting

Red food color

1 container chocolate creamy ready-to-spread frosting

Tray or cardboard (20×15 inches), covered with wrapping paper and plastic wrap, or foil

1 small round chocolate-covered creamy mint

1 Heat oven to 350°F (325°F for dark or nonstick pans). Grease 2 (9-inch) round cake pans with shortening or spray with cooking spray.

2 In large bowl, beat cake mix, water, oil and eggs with electric mixer on low speed 30 seconds, then on medium speed 2 minutes, scraping bowl occasionally. Divide batter between pans.

3 Bake as directed on box for 9-inch round pans. Cool 10 minutes. Remove cakes from pans to cooling racks. Cool completely, about 30 minutes. For easier handling, refrigerate or freeze cakes 30 to 60 minutes or until firm.

4 Meanwhile, in small bowl, tint ¼ cup vanilla frosting with red food color to make pink; place in resealable freezer plastic bag. Place ½ cup chocolate frosting in another resealable freezer plastic bag. Cut small tip off 1 corner of each bag. In medium bowl, stir together remaining vanilla frosting and chocolate frosting to make light brown frosting.

5 Using serrated knife, cut off rounded top of each cake to make level. Turn cakes cut side down. Cut cakes as shown in diagram. On tray, arrange cake pieces as shown in diagram, attaching pieces to each other and to tray with small amount of light brown frosting. Spread thin layer of light brown frosting over entire cake to seal in crumbs. Refrigerate or freeze cake 30 to 60 minutes to set frosting.

6 Frost entire cake with light brown frosting. With pink frosting, pipe on blanket; spread with metal spatula to make smooth. With darker chocolate frosting, pipe number on blanket. Pipe on hooves; spread to make smooth. Pipe on mane and tail, leaving in long strands to look like hair. Attach mint for eye. Store cake loosely covered.

1 Serving (Cake and Frosting Only): Calories 440; Total Fat 19g (Saturated Fat 4.5g, Trans Fat 4.5g); Cholesterol 35mg; Sodium 360mg; Total Carbohydrate 68g (Dietary Fiber 0g); Protein 1g **Exchanges:** 1 Starch, 3½ Other Carbohydrate, 3½ Fat **Carbohydrate Choices:** 4½

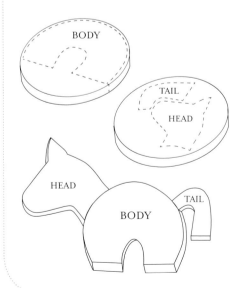

Silly Monster Cake

PREP TIME: 35 Minutes • **START TO FINISH: 3 Hours 35 Minutes** • **12 servings**

1 box yellow cake mix with pudding

Water, vegetable oil and eggs called for on cake mix box

3 containers creamy white or vanilla whipped ready-to-spread frosting

Neon orange food color

2 rolls berry-flavored chewy fruit snack (from 5-oz box)

3 to 4 pieces black string licorice

Small black gumdrop

2 sugar-style ice cream cones with pointed ends

2 wooden skewers (4 inch)

sweet tip

Make smaller monsters in cupcake form. Frost the cupcakes thickly with orange frosting, place a purchased candy eyeball in center and pipe a mouth with black decorating gel.

1 Heat oven to 350°F (325°F for dark or nonstick pans). Grease bottoms and sides of 2 (8-inch) round cake pans with shortening or spray with cooking spray.

2 Make and bake cake mix as directed on box for 8-inch round pans, using water, oil and eggs. Cool 10 minutes; remove from pans to cooling racks. Cool completely, about 1 hour. For easier handling, refrigerate or freeze cakes 30 minutes to 1 hour or until firm.

3 In medium bowl, mix 2 containers frosting and neon orange food color. On serving plate, place 1 cake layer, rounded side down. Spread with 1 cup of the orange frosting. Top with second cake layer, rounded side up. Spread thin layer of orange frosting over cake to seal in crumbs. Refrigerate or freeze 30 minutes to 1 hour to set frosting.

4 Frost top and side of cake with orange frosting, using back of spoon to create texture.

5 Spread large circle of vanilla frosting for eyeball. Unroll 1 fruit snack; cut out small circle for eye and teeth for mouth. Place circle in center of eye. Top with gumdrop. Spread vanilla frosting for mouth; add fruit snack for teeth. Outline each with black licorice; add eyelashes.

6 Unroll remaining fruit snack; wrap around ice cream cone. Insert skewers at top of cake; attach cones to look like horns.

1 Serving: Calories 710 (Calories from Fat 250); Total Fat 28g (Saturated Fat 6g, Trans Fat 7g); Cholesterol 45mg; Sodium 530mg; Potassium 85mg; Total Carbohydrate 112g (Dietary Fiber 0g); Protein 2g **Exchanges:** 1 Starch, 6½ Other Carbohydrate, 5½ Fat **Carbohydrate Choices:** 7½

Space Shuttle Cake

PREP TIME: 1 Hour • **START TO FINISH: 3 Hours 15 Minutes** • **15 servings**

CAKE

1 box yellow cake mix with pudding

Water, vegetable oil and eggs called for on cake mix box

Tray or cardboard (17×12 inches), covered with wrapping paper and plastic wrap, or foil

FROSTING AND DECORATIONS

2 containers vanilla creamy ready-to-spread frosting

Red licorice string

Red and blue miniature candy-coated chocolate baking bits

2 red gumdrop stars

3 small candy stars

6 soft red round candies

1 tube (0.68 oz) black decorating gel

3 candles

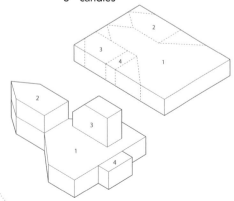

1 Heat oven to 350°F (325°F for dark or nonstick pan). Grease bottom and sides of 13×9-inch pan with shortening or spray with cooking spray.

2 Make and bake cake as directed on box for 13×9-inch pan, using water, oil and eggs. Cool 10 minutes. Remove cake from pan to cooling rack. Cool completely, about 1 hour. Refrigerate or freeze cake 1 hour or until firm.

3 Using serrated knife, cut rounded dome from top of cake to make flat surface; place cake cut side down. Cut cake as shown in diagram.

4 On tray, place cake piece #1. Arrange pieces #2, #3 and #4 as shown in diagram, trimming to fit, standing up piece #3 for top fin. Trim point of piece #2 for nose of shuttle. Attach each piece with a small amount of frosting.

5 Frost cake with a thin layer of frosting to seal in crumbs. Freeze 30 to 45 minutes to set frosting. Add final coat of frosting to cake, using up remaining frosting.

6 Use licorice to make diagonal lines across nose of shuttle and to outline top fin. Use baking bits to outline tip, wings and back of shuttle. Add large and small stars to wings and back; add round candies to both sides of fin. Write "USA" or another message on top of fin with decorating gel. Insert candles at end of shuttle. If desired, just before serving, light candles for "liftoff." Store cake loosely covered.

1 Serving (Cake and Frosting Only): Calories 410; Total Fat 17g (Saturated Fat 3.5g, Trans Fat 3.5g); Cholesterol 40mg; Sodium 320mg; Total Carbohydrate 62g (Dietary Fiber 0g); Protein 1g **Exchanges:** ½ Starch, 3½ Other Carbohydrate, 3½ Fat **Carbohydrate Choices:** 4

sweet tip

Place strips of waxed paper under corners of unfrosted cake pieces to catch frosting drips. After frosting, just remove the waxed paper strips.

Flip-Flops Cake

PREP TIME: 45 Minutes • **START TO FINISH:** 4 Hours 20 Minutes • **15 servings**

1 box yellow cake mix with pudding

Water, vegetable oil and eggs called for on cake mix box

Tray or cardboard, covered with wrapping paper and plastic wrap, or foil

2 containers vanilla whipped ready-to-spread frosting

Assorted food colors

About 40 small round candy-coated fruit-flavored chewy candies

1 roll chewy fruit snack (from 4.5-oz box)

2 silk daisy or edible pansy flowers

1 Heat oven to 350°F (325°F for dark or nonstick pans). Grease bottom and sides of 13×9-inch pan with shortening or spray with cooking spray.

2 Make and bake cake as directed on box for 13×9-inch pan, using water, oil and eggs. Cool 10 minutes. Remove from pan to cooling rack. Cool completely, about 1 hour. Refrigerate or freeze cake 1 hour or until firm.

3 In small bowl, mix 1 container frosting with food color to make desired color for sides of flip-flops. Reserve ⅓ cup frosting from second container. In small bowl, stir second food color into 1 cup of the remaining frosting to make desired color for tops of flip-flops.

4 Using serrated knife, cut rounded top off cake to level surface; place cut side down. Cut cake lengthwise in half. Continue cutting each piece to form flip-flop shape as shown in diagram. Place pieces on tray. Spread a thin layer of frosting for "sides" over each entire flip-flop to seal in crumbs. Refrigerate or freeze cake 30 to 60 minutes to set frosting.

5 Frost sides of flip-flops with the same remaining frosting. Frost tops of flip-flops with second color frosting.

6 Tint reserved ⅓ cup frosting with food color. To pipe frosting around top edge of flip-flops, spoon tinted frosting into small resealable freezer plastic bag; cut small tip off 1 bottom corner of bag. Pipe zigzag design. Place small candies around side edge of each flip-flop to look like jewels. Cut 2 (6-inch) pieces from fruit roll; cut pieces lengthwise in half. Arrange on flip-flops for straps. Just before serving, top with flowers. Store cake loosely covered.

1 Serving: Calories 350; Total Fat 17g (Saturated Fat 4.5g, Trans Fat 3g); Cholesterol 35mg; Sodium 220mg; Total Carbohydrate 47g (Dietary Fiber 0g); Protein 1g **Exchanges:** ½ Starch, 2½ Other Carbohydrate, 3½ Fat **Carbohydrate Choices:** 3

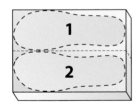

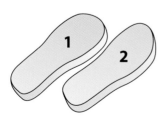

sweet tip

You can use paste food color to get more intense colors without diluting the frosting.

Inchworm Cake

PREP TIME: 30 Minutes • **START TO FINISH: 2 Hours 30 Minutes** • **16 servings**

1 box cake mix with pudding (any flavor)

Water, vegetable oil and eggs or egg whites called for on cake mix box

Green liquid food color

1½ containers vanilla creamy ready-to-spread frosting

Tray or cardboard (19×14 inches), covered with wrapping paper and plastic wrap, or foil

5 candy-coated chocolate candies

2 vanilla wafer cookies

2 small pretzel sticks

24 gumdrops

1 Heat oven to 350°F (325°F for dark or nonstick pan). Grease bottom and sides of 12-cup fluted tube cake pan with shortening.

2 Make, bake and cool cake as directed on box for 12-cup fluted tube cake pan, using water, oil and eggs or egg whites.

3 Cut cake as shown in diagram A. Freeze pieces uncovered 1 hour for easier frosting. Stir 8 drops food color into frosting. Arrange cake pieces on tray to form inchworm as shown in diagram B. Frost cake, attaching pieces with frosting.

4 Attach 1 chocolate candy to each vanilla wafer with frosting; attach to end of cake for eyes. Press 3 candies into frosting for mouth. Gently push 1 pretzel stick into flat end of gumdrop; repeat. Insert pretzel sticks into cake for antennae. Arrange remaining gumdrops along edge for feet. Store cake loosely covered.

1 Serving: Calories 340; Total Fat 15g (Saturated Fat 3g, Trans Fat 2.5g); Cholesterol 40mg; Sodium 290mg; Total Carbohydrate 51g (Dietary Fiber 0g); Protein 1g **Exchanges:** ½ Starch, 3 Other Carbohydrate, 3 Fat **Carbohydrate Choices:** 3½

sweet tip

Paste food color will produce more vividly colored frosting.

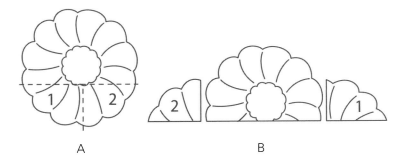

A   B

Neapolitan Confetti Cake

PREP TIME: 1 Hour 30 Minutes • **START TO FINISH:** 3 Hours 15 Minutes • **20 servings**

CAKE

4	cups all-purpose flour
6	teaspoons baking powder
1	teaspoon salt
1½	cups milk
2	teaspoons vanilla
1	teaspoon almond extract
9	egg whites
1¼	cups butter, softened
2½	cups granulated sugar
½	cup chopped fresh strawberries
	Pink paste food color, if desired
4	oz semisweet baking chocolate, melted, cooled

FROSTING AND GARNISH

3	containers fluffy white whipped ready-to-spread frosting
½	cup seedless strawberry jam
	Pink paste food color
	Powdered sugar
3	oz chocolate-flavored rolled fondant (from 24-oz box)
6	oz white rolled fondant (from 24-oz box)

1 Heat oven to 350°F. Grease bottoms and sides of 3 (9-inch) round cake pans with shortening; lightly flour.

2 In small bowl, mix flour, baking powder and salt. In medium bowl, stir milk, vanilla, almond extract and egg whites with whisk until well blended. In large bowl, beat butter and sugar with electric mixer on medium speed 5 minutes or until light and fluffy. Add flour mixture alternately with milk mixture, beating on low speed after each addition just until smooth.

3 Pour one-third of batter (about 3¼ cups) into 1 cake pan. In small bowl, mix one-third of batter, the strawberries and desired amount of pink food color. Pour into second cake pan. Stir melted chocolate into remaining batter. Pour into third cake pan.

4 Bake 30 to 35 minutes or until toothpick inserted in center comes out clean. Cool 10 minutes. Remove cakes from pans to cooling racks. Cool completely, about 1 hour.

5 In large bowl, stir frosting and jam until blended and smooth. Mix in desired amount of pink food color until blended. Brush off all loose crumbs from cake layers. Place chocolate cake layer, bottom side up, on serving plate; spread with about 1 cup frosting. Top with white cake layer, bottom side down; spread with about 1 cup frosting. Top with strawberry cake layer, bottom side down. Spread very thin layer of frosting on side of cake to seal in crumbs. Spread remaining frosting on side and top of cake.

6 Sprinkle work surface with powdered sugar. On work surface, knead chocolate fondant 8 to 10 times. Roll fondant to ⅛-inch thickness. Cut out ¾-inch rounds, 1-inch rounds and 1¼-inch rounds with assorted cutters. Place on cake. On work surface, knead pink paste food color into 3 oz of the white fondant until desired shade of pink. Roll fondant to ⅛-inch thickness. Cut out ¾-inch rounds, 1-inch rounds and 1¼-inch rounds. Repeat with remaining 3 oz white fondant and pink paste food color until pale pink. Cut out assorted rounds. Place on cake.

1 Serving: Calories 640; Total Fat 26g (Saturated Fat 13g, Trans Fat 3.5g); Cholesterol 30mg; Sodium 460mg; Total Carbohydrate 96g (Dietary Fiber 2g); Protein 5g **Exchanges:** 1½ Starch, 5 Other Carbohydrate, 5 Fat **Carbohydrate Choices:** 6½

Rainbow Angel Birthday Cake

PREP TIME: **20 Minutes** • START TO FINISH: **3 Hours** • **12 servings**

1 box white angel food cake mix

1¼ cups cold water

1 teaspoon grated lemon or orange peel

Red, yellow and green liquid food colors

1 cup vanilla creamy ready-to-spread frosting (from 1-lb container)

12 to 15 square candy fruit chews

sweet tip

For the best results, use a serrated knife for cutting angel food cakes.

1 Move oven rack to lowest position (remove other racks). Heat oven to 350°F.

2 In extra-large glass or metal bowl, beat cake mix, water and lemon peel with electric mixer on low speed 30 seconds; beat on medium speed 1 minute.

3 Divide batter evenly among 3 bowls. Gently stir 6 to 8 drops of one food color into each of the batters. Pour red batter into ungreased 10-inch angel food (tube) cake pan. (Do not use fluted tube cake pan or 9-inch angel food pan or batter will overflow.) Spoon yellow batter over red batter. Spoon green batter over top.

4 Bake 37 to 47 minutes or until top is dark golden brown and cracks feel very dry and not sticky. Do not underbake. Immediately turn pan upside down onto heatproof bottle or funnel until cake is completely cool, about 2 hours. Run knife around edges of cake; remove from pan to serving plate.

5 Spoon ½ cup of the frosting into microwavable bowl. Microwave uncovered on High about 15 seconds or until frosting can be stirred smooth and is thin enough to drizzle. (Or spoon frosting into 1-quart saucepan and heat over low heat, stirring constantly, until thin enough to drizzle.) Drizzle over cake.

6 Place remaining frosting in decorating bag with writing tip. Pipe a ribbon and bow on each candy square to look like a wrapped package. Arrange packages on top of cake. Store cake loosely covered at room temperature.

1 Serving (Cake and Frosting Only): Calories 240; Total Fat 5g (Saturated Fat 2g, Trans Fat 0g); Cholesterol 0mg; Sodium 370mg; Total Carbohydrate 45g (Dietary Fiber 0g); Protein 3g **Exchanges:** 1 Starch, 2 Other Carbohydrate, 1 Fat **Carbohydrate Choices:** 3

Polka Dot Cake

PREP TIME: 25 Minutes • **START TO FINISH:** 2 Hours 5 Minutes • **12 servings**

1 box white cake mix with pudding

Water, vegetable oil and egg whites called for on cake mix box

1 container fluffy white whipped ready-to-spread frosting

Red food color

½ cup round pink and orange candy melts or coating wafers (3 oz)

1 Heat oven to 350°F (325°F for dark or nonstick pans). Spray bottoms and sides of 2 (9- or 8-inch) round cake pans with baking spray with flour.

2 Make, bake and cool cake mix as directed on box for 9- or 8-inch round pans, using water, oil and egg whites.

3 Tint ⅓ cup of the frosting with 1 or 2 drops food color for desired shade of pink.

4 On serving plate, place 1 cake layer, rounded side down; spread pink frosting over layer almost to edge. Top with second layer, rounded side up. Frost side and top of cake with remaining white frosting.

5 Insert candies into frosting on side and top of cake as desired. Store cake loosely covered.

1 Serving: Calories 360; Total Fat 16g (Saturated Fat 5g, Trans Fat 2g); Cholesterol 0mg; Sodium 320mg; Total Carbohydrate 53g (Dietary Fiber 0g); Protein 2g **Exchanges:** 1 Starch, 2½ Other Carbohydrate, 3 Fat **Carbohydrate Choices:** 3½

Chocolate–Cherry Cola Cake

PREP TIME: 30 Minutes • **START TO FINISH: 2 Hours 15 Minutes** • **12 servings**

1 jar (10 oz) maraschino cherries, drained, ¼ cup liquid reserved

1 box devil's food cake mix with pudding

1 cup cherry cola carbonated beverage

½ cup vegetable oil

3 eggs

1 container vanilla whipped ready-to-spread frosting

1 cup marshmallow creme

24 additional maraschino cherries with stems, well drained, if desired

1 Heat oven to 350°F (325°F for dark or nonstick pan). Spray bottom only of 13×9-inch pan with baking spray with flour.

2 Chop cherries from 1 (10-oz) jar; set aside. In large bowl, beat cake mix, cola beverage, oil, eggs and ¼ cup reserved cherry liquid with electric mixer on low speed 30 seconds, then on medium speed 2 minutes, scraping bowl occasionally. Stir in chopped cherries. Pour into pan.

3 Bake 34 to 42 minutes or until toothpick inserted in center comes out clean. Cool completely, about 1 hour.

4 In small bowl, mix frosting and marshmallow creme until smooth. Frost cake. Top each piece with 2 cherries with stems. Store cake loosely covered.

1 Serving: Calories 430; Total Fat 18g (Saturated Fat 4.5g, Trans Fat 2g); Cholesterol 55mg; Sodium 350mg; Total Carbohydrate 65g (Dietary Fiber 1g); Protein 3g **Exchanges:** 1 Starch, 3½ Other Carbohydrate, 3½ Fat **Carbohydrate Choices:** 4

sweet tip

For chocolate-dipped cherries, melt ¼ cup semisweet chocolate chips and 1 teaspoon shortening in the microwave; stir. Dip well-drained cherries with stems into chocolate; refrigerate to set.

Chocolate Malt Ice Cream Cake

PREP TIME: 30 Minutes • **START TO FINISH:** 7 Hours 5 Minutes • **16 servings**

1½ cups all-purpose flour

1 cup sugar

¼ cup unsweetened baking cocoa

1 teaspoon baking soda

½ teaspoon salt

⅓ cup vegetable oil

1 teaspoon white vinegar

1 teaspoon vanilla

1 cup water

1¼ cups chocolate fudge topping

1½ quarts (6 cups) vanilla ice cream, slightly softened

2 cups malted milk ball candies, coarsely chopped

1 cup whipping cream

¼ cup chocolate fudge topping

Additional malted milk ball candies, if desired

1 Heat oven to 350°F. Grease bottom and side of 9- or 10-inch springform pan with shortening; lightly flour.

2 In large bowl, stir together flour, sugar, cocoa, baking soda and salt. Add oil, vinegar, vanilla and water; stir vigorously about 1 minute or until well blended. Immediately pour into pan.

3 Bake 30 to 35 minutes or until toothpick inserted in center comes out clean. Cool completely, about 1 hour.

4 Spread 1 cup of the fudge topping over cake. Freeze about 1 hour or until topping is firm.

5 Mix ice cream and coarsely chopped candies; spread over cake. Freeze about 4 hours or until ice cream is firm.

6 In chilled medium bowl, beat whipping cream with electric mixer on high speed until stiff peaks form. Remove side of pan; place cake on serving plate. Top with whipped cream. Melt remaining ¼ cup fudge topping; drizzle over whipped cream. Garnish with additional candies.

1 Serving: Calories 440; Total Fat 19g (Saturated Fat 10g, Trans Fat 0.5g); Cholesterol 40mg; Sodium 260mg; Total Carbohydrate 63g (Dietary Fiber 1g); Protein 4g **Exchanges:** 1½ Starch, 2½ Other Carbohydrate, 3½ Fat **Carbohydrate Choices:** 4

"Let's Party" Cake

PREP TIME: 30 Minutes • **START TO FINISH: 1 Hour 45 Minutes** • **12 servings**

1 box yellow cake mix with pudding (or any other flavor)

Water, vegetable oil and eggs called for on cake mix box

1 container fluffy white whipped or vanilla creamy ready-to-spread frosting

Yellow and red food colors

Blue and green neon food colors

3 packages (2.17 oz each) candy-coated tropical fruit–flavored chewy candies or 1 bag (8 oz) candy-coated chocolate candies

sweet tip
You can freeze the unfrosted cake and cupcakes (tightly covered) for up to 2 months.

1 Heat oven to 350°F (325°F for dark or nonstick pans). Grease bottom and side of 9-inch round cake pan with shortening, then lightly flour, or spray pan with baking spray with flour. Place paper baking cup in each of 12 regular-size muffin cups.

2 Make cake batter as directed on box, using water, oil and eggs. Spread half of batter in round pan; divide remaining batter evenly among muffin cups. Bake as directed on box. Cool 10 minutes; remove from pans to cooling racks. Cool completely, about 1 hour.

3 In small bowl, place 1 tablespoon frosting; stir in 2 drops yellow food color. In another small bowl, place ¼ cup frosting, 3 drops yellow food color and 1 drop red food color; stir to make orange frosting. In third small bowl, place ½ cup frosting; stir in 7 drops blue neon food color. To remaining frosting in container, stir in 7 drops green neon food color.

4 Trim off rounded top of cake layer; place on serving plate, cut side down. Frost top and side with green frosting. Frost 7 cupcakes with blue frosting, 4 cupcakes with orange frosting and 1 cupcake with yellow frosting. Place 1 blue cupcake on center of green frosted cake. Place remaining blue cupcakes, sides touching, in circle around center cupcake. Place 2 rows of 2 orange cupcakes on top center of blue cupcakes. Place yellow cupcake on top center. Press candies into frosting to decorate. Store cake loosely covered at room temperature.

1 Serving (1 slice of cake and 1 cupcake): Calories 420; Total Fat 18g (Saturated Fat 4.5g, Trans Fat 2g); Cholesterol 55mg; Sodium 310mg; Total Carbohydrate 61g (Dietary Fiber 0g); Protein 2g **Exchanges:** 1 Starch, 3 Other Carbohydrate, 3½ Fat **Carbohydrate Choices:** 4

Lucky Charms Cupcakes

PREP TIME: 35 Minutes • START TO FINISH: 1 Hour 40 Minutes • 24 cupcakes

1 box yellow or devil's food cake mix with pudding

Water, vegetable oil and eggs called for on cake mix box

1 container vanilla creamy ready-to-spread frosting

3 cups Lucky Charms® cereal

Green edible glitter

1 Heat oven to 350°F (325°F for dark or nonstick pans). Place paper baking cup in each of 24 regular-size muffin cups.

2 Make and bake cake mix as directed on box for 24 cupcakes, using water, oil and eggs. Cool in pans 10 minutes. Remove from pans to cooling rack. Cool completely, about 30 minutes.

3 Frost cupcakes with frosting. Top each cupcake with 2 tablespoons cereal; sprinkle with glitter. Store cupcakes loosely covered.

1 Cupcake: Calories 210; Total Fat 9g (Saturated Fat 2g, Trans Fat 1g); Cholesterol 25mg; Sodium 210mg; Total Carbohydrate 31g (Dietary Fiber 0g); Protein 1g **Exchanges:** 2 Other Carbohydrate, 2 Fat **Carbohydrate Choices:** 2

sweet tip

If you have only one pan and a recipe calls for more cupcakes than your pan will make, cover and refrigerate the rest of the batter while baking the first batch. Cool the pan about 15 minutes, then bake the rest of the batter, adding 1 to 2 minutes to the bake time.

Birthday Cupcakes

PREP TIME: 10 Minutes • **START TO FINISH: 1 Hour 40 Minutes** • **24 cupcakes**

1   box yellow cake mix with pudding

Water, vegetable oil and eggs called for on cake mix box

1   container creamy ready-to-spread frosting (any flavor)

24   ring-shaped hard candies or jelly bean candies, if desired

1 Heat oven to 350°F (325°F for dark or nonstick pans). Place paper baking cup in each of 24 regular-size muffin cups.

2 Make and bake cake mix as directed on box for 24 cupcakes, using water, oil and eggs. Cool in pans 10 minutes. Remove from pans to cooling rack. Cool completely, about 30 minutes.

3 Frost cupcakes with frosting. Decorate with candies. Store cupcakes loosely covered.

1 Cupcake: Calories 190; Total Fat 9g (Saturated Fat 2g, Trans Fat 1g); Cholesterol 25mg; Sodium 180mg; Total Carbohydrate 28g (Dietary Fiber 0g); Protein 1g **Exchanges:** ½ Starch, 1½ Other Carbohydrate, 1½ Fat **Carbohydrate Choices:** 2

sweet tip

For those who love chocolate, chocolate cake mix and chocolate frosting are perfect! Sprinkling with miniature chocolate chips and drizzling with melted white chocolate turns these simple cupcakes into bakery delights!

Cupcake Sliders

PREP TIME: 1 Hour 40 Minutes • **START TO FINISH:** 3 Hours 20 Minutes • **64 cupcake sliders**

CUPCAKES

2⅓	cups all-purpose flour
2½	teaspoons baking powder
½	teaspoon salt
1	cup butter, softened
1¼	cups sugar
3	eggs
1	teaspoon vanilla
⅔	cup milk

BROWNIES

1	box (1 lb 2.3 oz) fudge brownie mix
¼	cup water
⅔	cup vegetable oil
2	eggs

TOPPINGS

1½	cups flaked coconut
	Green liquid food color
4	to 6 drops water
1	cup chocolate creamy ready-to-spread frosting (from 1-lb container)
64	square orange candy fruit chews, unwrapped
16	rolls strawberry chewy fruit snack in 3-foot rolls (from three 4.5-oz boxes), unwrapped
2	tablespoons honey
1	to 2 teaspoons water
2	tablespoons sesame seeds

1 Heat oven to 350°F. Place mini paper baking cup in each of 24 mini muffin cups. In medium bowl, mix flour, baking powder and salt; set aside. In large bowl, beat butter with electric mixer on medium speed 30 seconds. Gradually add sugar, about ¼ cup at a time, beating well after each addition. Beat 2 minutes longer. Add 3 eggs, one at a time, beating well after each addition. Beat in vanilla. On low speed, alternately add flour mixture, about one-third at a time, and milk, about half at a time, beating just until blended. Fill each cup with about 1 tablespoon plus 1 teaspoon batter or until about two-thirds full. (Cover and refrigerate remaining batter until ready to bake; cool pan 15 minutes before reusing.)

2 Bake 17 to 20 minutes or until golden brown and toothpick inserted in center comes out clean. Cool 5 minutes. Remove cupcakes from pans to cooling racks. Cool completely, about 15 minutes. Repeat with remaining batter to make an additional 48 mini cupcakes. Leave oven temperature at 350°F. Grease 15×10×1-inch pan with shortening or spray with cooking spray. In large bowl, stir brownie mix, ¼ cup water, the oil and 2 eggs with spoon until blended. Pour into pan.

3 Bake 22 to 26 minutes or until toothpick inserted 2 inches from side of pan comes out almost clean. Cool 20 minutes. With 1½-inch round cutter, cut 64 brownie rounds for "burgers." In medium bowl, toss coconut, 4 to 6 drops food color and 4 to 6 drops water with fork until coconut reaches desired color; set aside.

4 Remove paper baking cups from 64 cupcakes (reserve remaining cupcakes for another use). Cut each cupcake horizontally in half to make tops and bottoms of "buns." Place brownie rounds (burgers) on bottom halves of cupcakes (buns), using frosting to secure.

5 To make "cheese slices," on large microwavable plate, microwave about 8 orange candies at a time uncovered on High 5 to 10 seconds to soften. Use bottom of measuring cup to flatten until each is about 1¾ inches in diameter. Secure to "burgers" with frosting. Repeat to make additional "cheese slices."

6 To make "ketchup," cut chewy fruit snack rolls with kitchen scissors into about 1¾-inch irregular-edged rounds. Secure to "cheese" with frosting. Spread dab of frosting on "ketchup"; sprinkle each slider with slightly less than 2 teaspoons tinted coconut for "shredded lettuce."

7 In small bowl, mix honey and enough of the 1 to 2 teaspoons water until thin consistency. Brush honey mixture lightly over "bun tops"; sprinkle each with sesame seeds. Spread dab of frosting on cut sides of "bun tops"; secure to coconut, frosting side down.

1 Cupcake Slider: Calories 190; Total Fat 8g (Saturated Fat 3.5g, Trans Fat 0g); Cholesterol 25mg; Sodium 135mg; Total Carbohydrate 27g (Dietary Fiber 0g); Protein 1g **Exchanges:** ½ Starch, 1½ Other Carbohydrate, 1½ Fat **Carbohydrate Choices:** 2

sweet tip

For a fun touch, serve these "sliders" in red and white checked paper food trays, like at a fast-food restaurant, accompanied by "fries" (yellow licorice twists).

Banana Split Cupcakes

PREP TIME: 25 Minutes • **START TO FINISH: 1 Hour 45 Minutes** • **48 mini cupcakes**

1 box yellow cake mix with pudding

1 cup mashed very ripe bananas (2 medium)

½ cup vegetable oil

¼ cup water

3 eggs

1 container chocolate creamy ready-to-spread frosting

1 container vanilla or creamy white creamy ready-to-spread frosting

1 container strawberry whipped ready-to-spread frosting

48 maraschino cherries with stems, patted dry

¼ cup multicolored candy sprinkles

1 Heat oven to 350°F. Place mini paper baking cup in each of 24 mini muffin cups.

2 In large bowl, beat cake mix, bananas, oil, water and eggs with electric mixer on low speed 30 seconds. Beat on medium speed 2 minutes. Fill each muffin cup two-thirds full. (Cover and refrigerate remaining batter until ready to bake.)

3 Bake 15 minutes or until toothpick inserted in center comes out clean. Cool 5 minutes. Remove from pans to cooling racks. Cool completely, about 15 minutes. Repeat with remaining batter to make 24 more mini cupcakes.

4 In small microwavable bowl, reserve ¼ cup of the chocolate frosting. Spoon remaining frosting into decorating bag fitted with large star tip #7. Pipe frosting onto 16 cupcakes. Repeat with white and strawberry frosting.

5 Microwave reserved chocolate frosting uncovered on High 20 to 25 seconds or until smooth. Cool 1 minute; drizzle over frosting on each cupcake. Pipe dab of white frosting on each; top with 1 cherry and candy sprinkles.

1 Mini Cupcake: Calories 180; Total Fat 7g (Saturated Fat 2g, Trans Fat 1.5g); Cholesterol 10mg; Sodium 120mg; Total Carbohydrate 27g (Dietary Fiber 0g); Protein 0g **Exchanges:** 2 Other Carbohydrate, 1½ Fat **Carbohydrate Choices:** 2

Somewhere-Over-the-Rainbow Cupcakes

PREP TIME: 40 Minutes • **START TO FINISH: 1 Hour 40 Minutes** • **12 cupcakes**

CUPCAKES

1½	cups all-purpose flour
1¾	teaspoons baking powder
½	cup butter, softened
1	cup granulated sugar
2	eggs
1	teaspoon vanilla
1	teaspoon coconut extract
¾	cup canned coconut milk (not cream of coconut)
	Yellow, green, red and blue liquid food color

FROSTING

1½	cups unsalted butter, softened
6	cups powdered sugar
	Dash salt
5	tablespoons milk
½	teaspoon vanilla
¼	teaspoon coconut extract
	Jumbo multicolored candy sprinkles, if desired

1 Cupcake: Calories 690; Total Fat 35g (Saturated Fat 22g, Trans Fat 1g); Cholesterol 115mg; Sodium 160mg; Total Carbohydrate 90g (Dietary Fiber 0g); Protein 3g **Exchanges:** 1 Starch, 5 Other Carbohydrate, 7 Fat **Carbohydrate Choices:** 6

1 Heat oven to 350°F. Place paper baking cup in each of 12 regular-size muffin cups.

2 In small bowl, stir flour and baking powder; set aside. In medium bowl, beat ½ cup butter and the granulated sugar with electric mixer on medium speed 2 minutes or until light and fluffy. Add eggs, one at a time, beating well after each addition. Beat in 1 teaspoon vanilla and 1 teaspoon coconut extract. On low speed, alternately add flour mixture, half at a time, and coconut milk, beating just until blended.

3 Measure about ¾ cup batter into each of 5 small bowls. Stir about 6 drops yellow food color into batter in first bowl. Tint second bowl green with 6 drops green food color, third bowl red with about 8 drops red food color, fourth bowl blue with about 10 drops blue food color and fifth bowl purple with about 8 drops red food color and 3 drops blue food color.

4 Spoon slightly less than 1 tablespoon of yellow batter into each cup; smooth to edge of baking cup with back of spoon. Repeat with green, red, blue and purple batters (cups should be about three-fourths full).

5 Bake 18 to 22 minutes or until toothpick inserted in center of cupcake comes out clean. Cool 5 minutes. Remove from pan to cooling rack. Cool completely, about 30 minutes.

6 In large bowl, beat 1½ cups butter, the powdered sugar and salt with electric mixer until light and fluffy. Beat in 4 tablespoons of the milk, ½ teaspoon vanilla and ¼ teaspoon coconut extract. Add remaining milk, 1 teaspoon at a time, until frosting is desired consistency. Beat until fluffy. Pipe or spread about ¼ cup frosting onto each cupcake. Sprinkle with candy sprinkles.

sweet tip

If your kids are not in love with coconut, substitute vanilla for the coconut extract in the cake and frosting.

Marshmallow Birthday Cupcakes

PREP TIME: 25 Minutes • **START TO FINISH:** 1 Hour 25 Minutes • **24 cupcakes**

CUPCAKES

1 box white cake mix with pudding

Water, vegetable oil and egg whites called for on cake mix box

FROSTING AND DECORATIONS

2 containers creamy white creamy ready-to-spread frosting

24 large marshmallows

Colored sugar or candy sprinkles

White or colored birthday candles

1 Heat oven to 350°F (325°F for dark or nonstick pans). Place paper baking cup in each of 24 regular-size muffin cups.

2 Make and bake cake mix as directed on box for cupcakes, using water, oil and egg whites. Cool completely, about 30 minutes.

3 Frost cooled cupcakes. For each cupcake, cut 1 marshmallow with dampened kitchen scissors into slices; sprinkle with colored sugar. Arrange on cupcakes in flower shape. Place candle in center of each flower.

1 Frosted Cupcake (Undecorated): Calories 300; Total Fat 9g (Saturated Fat 2g, Trans Fat 2g); Cholesterol 0mg; Sodium 240mg; Total Carbohydrate 52g (Dietary Fiber 0g); Protein 1g **Exchanges:** 3½ Other Carbohydrate, 2 Fat **Carbohydrate Choices:** 3½

sweet tips

Use edible glitter in place of the colored sugar or candy sprinkles. It adds sparkle to cake decorations.

Check out party-supply or cake-decorating stores for fun birthday candles. Lots of new and unique shapes are available.

"Hot" Chocolate Cake

PREP TIME: 25 Minutes • **START TO FINISH: 8 Hours 15 Minutes** • **24 servings**

CAKE

1½	cups sugar
1¼	cups vegetable oil
1¼	cups buttermilk
1½	teaspoons vanilla
2	eggs
2¼	cups all-purpose flour
⅓	cup unsweetened dark baking cocoa
2	teaspoons ground red pepper (cayenne)
1½	teaspoons baking powder
1½	teaspoons baking soda
¾	teaspoon salt
1¼	cups hot water or hot strong brewed coffee

SPICY BITTERSWEET GANACHE

10	oz bittersweet baking chocolate, chopped
1½	cups whipping cream
½	teaspoon ground red pepper (cayenne)

WHITE CHOCOLATE GANACHE

24	oz white chocolate baking bars or squares, chopped
1	cup whipping cream
1	tube (0.68 oz) red decorating gel

1 Heat oven to 350°F. Grease bottom and sides of 13×9-inch pan with shortening.

2 In large bowl, beat cake ingredients with electric mixer on low speed 30 seconds, scraping bowl often. Beat on medium speed 2 minutes longer, scraping bowl occasionally. Pour batter into pan.

3 Bake 30 to 35 minutes or until toothpick inserted in center comes out clean. Cool completely in pan on cooling rack, about 2 hours.

4 Place bittersweet chocolate in medium heatproof bowl; set aside. In 1-quart saucepan, heat 1½ cups whipping cream to simmering. Remove from heat; stir in ½ teaspoon red pepper. Let stand 10 minutes. Return whipping cream in saucepan to heat; heat to simmering. Pour over bittersweet chocolate. Let stand 2 minutes; stir until smooth. Spread ganache over cake. Refrigerate until set, about 1 hour.

5 Place white chocolate in medium heatproof bowl. In 1-quart saucepan, heat 1 cup whipping cream to boiling. Pour over white chocolate. Let stand 2 minutes; stir until smooth. Spread evenly over bittersweet ganache.

6 Drizzle decorating gel in rows over cake. Pull toothpick through rows in opposite direction to create swirled pattern. Refrigerate at least 4 hours or overnight.

1 Serving: Calories 540; Total Fat 37g (Saturated Fat 17g, Trans Fat 0g); Cholesterol 55mg; Sodium 240mg; Total Carbohydrate 45g (Dietary Fiber 3g); Protein 6g **Exchanges:** 2 Starch, 1 Other Carbohydrate, 7 Fat **Carbohydrate Choices:** 3

Cream-Filled Butter Pecan Birthday Cake

PREP TIME: 25 Minutes • **START TO FINISH: 2 Hours 10 Minutes** • **12 servings**

CAKE

- ½ cup butter
- ¼ cup whipping cream
- 1 cup packed brown sugar
- 1 box butter pecan cake mix with pudding
- 1 cup water
- ⅓ cup vegetable oil
- 3 eggs

TOPPING

- 1¾ cups whipping cream
- ¼ cup powdered sugar
- ¼ teaspoon vanilla
- ¼ cup chocolate-coated toffee bits

1 Heat oven to 325°F. Place sheet of waxed paper under cooling racks.

2 In 1-quart saucepan, heat butter, ¼ cup whipping cream and the brown sugar over low heat, stirring occasionally, just until butter is melted. Pour into 2 (9-inch) round cake pans (do not use dark or nonstick pans).

3 In large bowl, beat cake mix, water, oil and eggs with electric mixer on low speed 30 seconds, then on medium speed 2 minutes, scraping bowl occasionally. Carefully spoon half of cake batter into each pan, starting at outer edge and continuing toward center so brown sugar mixture does not get moved out to sides of pans.

4 Bake 30 to 37 minutes or until toothpick inserted in center comes out clean. Run knife around edge of cakes to loosen from pan; turn upside down onto cooling racks. Leave pans over cakes 1 minute before removing. Cool completely, about 1 hour.

5 In chilled medium bowl, beat 1¾ cups whipping cream, the powdered sugar and vanilla with electric mixer on high speed until stiff peaks form.

6 On serving tray, place 1 cake layer, brown sugar side up. Spread with half of the whipped cream. Top with second layer, brown sugar side up. Spread with remaining whipped cream. Sprinkle with toffee bits. Store cake covered in refrigerator.

1 Serving: Calories 530; Total Fat 33g (Saturated Fat 17g, Trans Fat 1g); Cholesterol 130mg; Sodium 350mg; Total Carbohydrate 55g (Dietary Fiber 0g); Protein 3g **Exchanges:** 1 Starch, 2½ Other Carbohydrate, 6½ Fat **Carbohydrate Choices:** 3½

Pink Almond Party Cake

PREP TIME: 40 Minutes   •   **START TO FINISH:** 2 Hours 20 Minutes   •   **12 servings**

CAKE

1	box white cake mix with pudding
	Water, vegetable oil and egg whites called for on cake mix box
2	teaspoons almond extract
6	drops red liquid food color

GARNISH

4	oz vanilla-flavored candy coating (almond bark), chopped
2	teaspoons vegetable oil
	Red liquid food color

FROSTING

½	cup butter, softened
¼	cup shortening
1	teaspoon almond extract
4	cups powdered sugar
4	to 5 tablespoons milk

sweet tip

Stir a teaspoon of almond extract into a container of fluffy white whipped ready-to-spread frosting for a fast and delicious frosting.

1 Heat oven to 350°F (325°F for dark or nonstick pan). Spray bottoms and sides of 2 (9- or 8-inch) round cake pans with baking spray with flour.

2 In large bowl, beat cake ingredients on low speed 30 seconds, then on medium speed 2 minutes, scraping bowl occasionally. Pour into pans.

3 Bake and cool as directed on box for 9- or 8-inch round pans.

4 Meanwhile, in small microwavable bowl, microwave candy coating uncovered on High 1 minute, stirring twice, until melted and smooth. Stir in 2 teaspoons oil. Spoon about half the melted coating into another bowl; stir in 2 to 3 drops food color to tint light pink.

5 Line 6-oz custard cup or other small bowl with foil. Pour half of the untinted coating into foil-lined bowl. Spoon half of the pink coating on top; pull a knife through coatings to make marbled design. Repeat with remaining untinted and tinted coatings, adding on top of marbled coatings. Refrigerate about 20 minutes or until set; remove from refrigerator. (If refrigerated longer, let stand at room temperature 10 minutes to soften.)

6 In large bowl, beat butter, shortening, 1 teaspoon almond extract, the powdered sugar and 4 tablespoons of the milk with electric mixer on low speed until well blended. Beat on medium speed, adding enough of the remaining 1 tablespoon milk until fluffy and spreadable.

7 Place 1 cake layer, rounded side down, on serving plate; frost top. Top with second layer, rounded side up. Frost side and top of cake.

8 Remove coating from bowl; peel off foil. With vegetable peeler, make curls by pulling peeler around outside edge of block of coating. Place curls on top of cake. Store cake loosely covered.

1 Serving: Calories 540; Total Fat 24g (Saturated Fat 10g, Trans Fat 1g); Cholesterol 25mg; Sodium 350mg; Total Carbohydrate 77g (Dietary Fiber 0g); Protein 3g **Exchanges:** 1 Starch, 4 Other Carbohydrate, 4½ Fat **Carbohydrate Choices:** 5

Chocolate Ganache Cake

PREP TIME: 25 Minutes • **START TO FINISH:** 3 Hours 15 Minutes • **16 servings**

1   box chocolate fudge
      cake mix with pudding

      Water, vegetable oil
      and eggs called for on
      cake mix box

1   container chocolate creamy
      ready-to-spread frosting

⅓   cup whipping cream

½   cup semisweet chocolate
      chips

2   bars (1.4 oz each) chocolate-
      covered toffee candy, very
      coarsely chopped

1   Heat oven to 350°F (325°F for dark or nonstick pans).

2   Make, bake and cool cake as directed on box for 2 (8- or 9-inch) round cake pans, using water, oil and eggs.

3   Place 1 cake layer, rounded side down, on serving plate. Spread with about ⅓ cup frosting. Top with second layer, rounded side up. Frost side and top of cake with remaining frosting.

4   In 1-quart saucepan, heat whipping cream over medium heat until hot (do not boil). Remove from heat. Stir in chocolate chips until melted and smooth. Let stand 5 minutes. Carefully pour chocolate mixture onto top center of cake; spread to edge, allowing some to drizzle down side. Garnish top of cake with toffee candy. Refrigerate about 1 hour or until chocolate is set. Store cake covered in refrigerator.

1 Serving: Calories 350; Total Fat 18g (Saturated Fat 6g, Trans Fat 2g); Cholesterol 50mg; Sodium 350mg; Total Carbohydrate 46g (Dietary Fiber 1g); Protein 3g **Exchanges:** 1 Starch, 2 Other Carbohydrate, 3½ Fat **Carbohydrate Choices:** 3

sweet tips

Ganache, the cream and chocolate mixture, is ready to use when it mounds slightly when dropped from a spoon. It will become firmer the longer it cools.

Glaze the cake on a rack with waxed paper under the rack; any extra drips of the ganache will fall onto the waxed paper. When the ganache hardens, you can easily and neatly transfer the cake to your serving plate.

Orange Crunch Cake

PREP TIME: 40 Minutes • **START TO FINISH: 2 Hours 45 Minutes** • **16 servings**

CAKE

1	cup graham cracker crumbs (15 squares)
½	cup packed brown sugar
½	cup chopped pecans
1	teaspoon ground cinnamon
½	cup butter, melted
1	box yellow cake mix with pudding
	Grated peel from 2 oranges (about 2 tablespoons)
	Juice from 2 oranges, plus water to measure 1 cup
⅓	cup vegetable oil
3	eggs

FROSTING AND GARNISH

1	container vanilla whipped ready-to-spread frosting
2	cups frozen (thawed) whipped topping
1	to 2 tablespoons grated orange peel
	Orange slices, if desired

sweet tip

For the freshest orange flavor, grate only the bright orange part of the peel. Stop at the bitter-tasting pith, the white portion directly under the bright orange part.

1 Heat oven to 350°F (dark or nonstick pans are not recommended). Grease bottoms only of 2 (8- or 9-inch) round cake pans with shortening. Line bottoms of pans with waxed paper, then grease and flour entire pans.

2 In medium bowl, mix cracker crumbs, brown sugar, pecans, cinnamon and butter. Sprinkle 1 cup pecan mixture evenly into bottom of each pan; press gently.

3 In large bowl, beat cake mix, orange peel, orange juice mixture, oil and eggs with electric mixer on low speed 30 seconds, then on medium speed 2 minutes, scraping bowl occasionally. Pour evenly into pans.

4 Bake 8-inch rounds 34 to 41 minutes, 9-inch rounds 30 to 37 minutes, or until toothpick inserted in center comes out clean and tops are a rich golden brown. Cool in pans 15 minutes. Carefully run sharp knife around sides of pans to loosen cakes. Remove from pans to cooling rack, placing crumb mixture side up. Cool completely, about 1 hour.

5 In large bowl, stir frosting ingredients until well blended. Place 1 layer, crumb side up, on serving plate. Spread with 1 cup frosting to within ¼ inch of edge. Add second layer, crumb side up. Frost side and top of cake with remaining frosting. Garnish with orange slices. To serve, cut cake with serrated knife. Store cake covered in refrigerator.

1 Serving: Calories 410; Total Fat 21g (Saturated Fat 8g, Trans Fat 1.5g); Cholesterol 50mg; Sodium 310mg; Total Carbohydrate 51g (Dietary Fiber 1g); Protein 2g **Exchanges:** ½ Starch, 3 Other Carbohydrate, 4 Fat **Carbohydrate Choices:** 3½

Lemon Cake with Whipped Cream Mousse

PREP TIME: 25 Minutes • **START TO FINISH: 2 Hours 10 Minutes** • **16 servings**

1 box white cake mix
  with pudding

  Water, vegetable oil and
  egg whites called for on
  cake mix box

2 cups whipping cream

¼ cup powdered sugar

1 jar (10 oz) lemon curd

2 teaspoons grated
  lemon peel

1 Heat oven to 350°F (325°F for dark or nonstick pans).

2 Make, bake and cool cake as directed on box for 2 (8- or 9-inch) round cake pans, using water, oil and egg whites.

3 In chilled medium bowl, beat whipping cream and powdered sugar with electric mixer on high speed until stiff peaks form. Fold in lemon curd and lemon peel.

4 Place 1 cake layer, rounded side down, on serving plate. Spread with 1 cup of the lemon mixture to within ¼ inch of edge. Top with second layer, rounded side up. Frost side and top of cake with remaining lemon mixture. Store cake loosely covered in refrigerator.

1 Serving: Calories 310; Total Fat 18g (Saturated Fat 9g, Trans Fat 0g); Cholesterol 55mg; Sodium 230mg; Total Carbohydrate 36g (Dietary Fiber 0g); Protein 2g **Exchanges:** ½ Starch, 2 Other Carbohydrate, 3½ Fat **Carbohydrate Choices:** 2½

sweet tip

Lemon curd is a rich, tart custard made with sugar, lemon juice, lemon peel, butter and eggs. Although you can make it from scratch, it's much easier to pick up a jar in the jams and jellies section of the supermarket.

Mojito Cake

PREP TIME: **30 Minutes** • START TO FINISH: **2 Hours 20 Minutes** • **15 servings**

CAKE

- 1 box white cake mix with pudding
- 1 cup unflavored carbonated water
- ⅓ cup vegetable oil
- ¼ cup rum or 1 teaspoon rum extract plus ¼ cup water
- 3 tablespoons chopped fresh mint leaves
- 2 teaspoons grated lime peel
- 3 egg whites

GLAZE

- ½ cup butter
- ¼ cup water
- 1 cup granulated sugar
- ½ cup rum or 2 teaspoons rum extract plus ½ cup water

GARNISH

- 1 cup whipping cream
- 2 tablespoons powdered sugar
- 15 fresh mint leaves, if desired

  Shredded lime peel, if desired

1 Heat oven to 350°F (325°F for dark or nonstick pan). Spray bottom only of 13×9-inch pan with baking spray with flour.

2 In large bowl, beat cake ingredients with electric mixer on low speed 30 seconds, then on medium speed 2 minutes, scraping bowl occasionally. Pour batter into pan.

3 Bake as directed on box for 13×9-inch pan. Cool 15 minutes.

4 Meanwhile, in 2-quart saucepan, mix glaze ingredients. Heat to boiling over high heat, stirring frequently. Reduce heat to medium; continue to boil 3 minutes, stirring frequently, until glaze has thickened slightly.

5 Poke warm cake every inch with fork tines. Pour glaze slowly over cake. Cool completely, about 1 hour.

6 In small bowl, beat whipping cream and powdered sugar with electric mixer on high speed until soft peaks form. Garnish each serving with whipped cream, mint leaf and shredded lime peel. Store cake loosely covered.

1 Serving: Calories 350; Total Fat 17g (Saturated Fat 8g, Trans Fat 0g); Cholesterol 35mg; Sodium 270mg; Total Carbohydrate 41g (Dietary Fiber 0g); Protein 2g **Exchanges:** ½ Starch, 2½ Other Carbohydrate, 3½ Fat **Carbohydrate Choices:** 3

sweet tip

A mojito typically refers to a cocktail made with lime juice, sugar, mint leaves and rum. We've taken those same flavors and turned them into a tasty cake.

Ultimate "24-Carat" Cake

PREP TIME: **20 Minutes** • START TO FINISH: **2 Hours 15 Minutes** • **12 servings**

1 box carrot cake mix with pudding

½ cup water

⅔ cup vegetable oil

4 eggs

1 can (8 oz) crushed pineapple in juice, undrained

½ cup chopped nuts

½ cup shredded coconut

½ cup raisins

1 container cream cheese creamy ready-to-spread frosting

1 Heat oven to 350°F (325°F for dark or nonstick pans). Grease bottoms only of 2 (8- or 9-inch) round cake pans with shortening, then lightly flour, or spray with baking spray with flour.

2 In large bowl, beat cake mix, water, oil, eggs and pineapple (with juice) with electric mixer on low speed 30 seconds, then on medium speed 2 minutes. Stir in nuts, coconut and raisins. Pour into pans.

3 Bake 8-inch rounds 40 to 45 minutes, 9-inch rounds 30 to 35 minutes, or until toothpick inserted in center comes out clean. Cool 10 minutes. Run knife around sides of pans to loosen cakes; remove from pans to cooling rack. Cool completely, about 1 hour.

4 Place 1 cake layer, rounded side down, on serving plate. Spread with about ⅓ cup frosting. Place second layer, rounded side up, on top. Frost side and top of cake with remaining frosting. Store cake covered in refrigerator.

1 Serving: Calories 500; Total Fat 25g (Saturated Fat 6g, Trans Fat 2g); Cholesterol 70mg; Sodium 370mg; Total Carbohydrate 65g (Dietary Fiber 1g); Protein 5g **Exchanges:** 1 Starch, 3½ Other Carbohydrate, 5 Fat **Carbohydrate Choices:** 4

sweet tip

Select your favorite type of nuts for this fabulous cake—pecans, walnuts, almonds or hazelnuts are all good choices.

Strawberry-Rhubarb Chiffon Cake

PREP TIME: **55 Minutes** • START TO FINISH: **3 Hours 55 Minutes** • **20 servings**

CAKE

1¾ cups all-purpose flour

2 teaspoons baking powder

1 teaspoon salt

1¼ cups granulated sugar

½ cup vegetable oil

6 eggs, separated

10 strawberries, pureed in blender or food processor (about ¾ cup)

Red liquid food color

½ teaspoon cream of tartar

FILLING AND GLAZE

1 cup frozen cut rhubarb, thawed and drained or chopped fresh rhubarb

2 teaspoons grated lemon peel

¼ cup granulated sugar

1 tablespoon water

1½ cups quartered strawberries

1 cup whipping cream

1½ cups powdered sugar

1 Heat oven to 350°F. In large bowl, mix flour, baking powder, salt and ½ cup of the granulated sugar until blended. Add oil, egg yolks, pureed strawberries and 22 drops food color; beat with electric mixer on medium speed about 2 minutes or until blended. Set aside.

2 Wash and dry beaters. In medium bowl, beat egg whites and cream of tartar with electric mixer on medium speed about 1 minute 30 seconds or until soft peaks form. Gradually add the remaining ¾ cup granulated sugar, beating until stiff peaks form. Fold one-third of the egg white mixture into the egg yolk batter gently but thoroughly. Fold in remaining egg white mixture. Pour into ungreased 10-inch angel food (tube) cake pan. Tap pan on counter to remove air bubbles.

3 Bake 50 to 60 minutes or until toothpick inserted in center comes out clean. Immediately turn pan upside down onto heatproof bottle or funnel. Let hang about 2 hours or until cake is completely cool.

4 Meanwhile, in 1-quart saucepan, heat rhubarb, lemon peel, ¼ cup granulated sugar and the water to boiling over medium heat. Reduce heat to medium-low; simmer until tender, about 3 minutes. Remove from heat; set aside to cool, about 30 minutes. Stir in quartered strawberries.

5 In medium bowl, beat ½ cup of the whipping cream and 1 tablespoon of the powdered sugar until stiff peaks form. Fold in ½ cup of the cooled strawberry-rhubarb mixture. Reserve remaining mixture for top of cake. Place cake top side down on serving platter. Cut 1-inch layer off top of cake; set aside. Cut tunnel into cake 1 inch deep and 1 inch wide; discard tunnel scraps. Fill tunnel with strawberry-rhubarb cream mixture. Replace top of cake.

6 In medium bowl, stir remaining ½ cup whipping cream and remaining powdered sugar (almost 1½ cups) until smooth. Spoon glaze over top of cake, letting it run down side. Top with reserved strawberry-rhubarb mixture just before serving. Store cake in refrigerator.

1 Serving: Calories 270; Total Fat 12g (Saturated Fat 4g, Trans Fat 0g); Cholesterol 70mg; Sodium 190mg; Total Carbohydrate 38g (Dietary Fiber 1g); Protein 3g **Exchanges:** 1 Starch, 1½ Other Carbohydrate, 2½ Fat **Carbohydrate Choices:** 2½

sweet tip

Rhubarb and strawberries are a refreshing pair for spring. To prepare fresh rhubarb, trim the ends and discard all traces of the leaves (rhubarb leaves are poisonous). Scrub the stalks and cut into pieces about 1 inch long.

Mexican Chocolate Cake with Caramel Cream Frosting

PREP TIME: 25 Minutes • **START TO FINISH:** 1 Hour 45 Minutes • **12 servings**

CAKE

- ¾ cup hot brewed coffee
- ½ cup unsweetened baking cocoa
- 3 teaspoons ground cinnamon
- 2 cups all-purpose flour
- 1 teaspoon baking powder
- ¾ teaspoon salt
- ½ teaspoon baking soda
- ¾ cup butter, softened
- 1¾ cups sugar
- 3 eggs
- ¾ cup buttermilk
- 2 teaspoons vanilla

FROSTING

- 1 can (13.4 oz) dulce de leche (caramelized sweetened condensed milk)
- 1 package (8 oz) cream cheese, softened
- ½ cup whipping cream

1 Heat oven to 350°F. Spray bottoms and sides of 2 (9-inch) round cake pans with cooking spray; line bottoms of pans with cooking parchment or waxed paper. In medium bowl, beat coffee, cocoa and cinnamon with whisk until smooth; set aside to cool slightly.

2 In another medium bowl, stir flour, baking powder, salt and baking soda; set aside. In large bowl, beat butter and sugar with electric mixer on high speed until creamy. Add eggs, one at a time, beating well after each addition; set aside.

3 Stir buttermilk and vanilla into coffee mixture. Starting with flour mixture, alternately beat flour mixture, one-third at a time, and coffee mixture, one-third at a time, into butter mixture on medium speed, scraping bowl occasionally. When all ingredients have been added, beat 30 to 60 seconds longer or until batter is smooth and well blended. Pour into pans.

4 Bake 32 to 37 minutes or until toothpick inserted near center comes out clean and cake springs back when touched lightly in center. Cool in pans on cooling racks 10 minutes. Remove cakes from pans to cooling racks (leave paper on cakes). Cool completely, about 30 minutes.

5 In large bowl, beat dulce de leche and cream cheese with electric mixer on high speed about 2 minutes or until blended and smooth; scrape side of bowl. Beat in whipping cream until stiff peaks form.

6 On serving plate, place 1 cake layer, rounded side down; remove paper. Spread ¾ cup of frosting over top to within ½ inch of edge. Remove paper from second cake layer; place, rounded side up, on first cake layer. Frost side and top of cake with remaining frosting. Serve cake immediately, or refrigerate until serving.

1 Serving: Calories 530; Total Fat 25g (Saturated Fat 15g, Trans Fat 1g); Cholesterol 115mg; Sodium 450mg; Total Carbohydrate 67g (Dietary Fiber 2g); Protein 9g **Exchanges:** ½ Starch, 4 Other Carbohydrate, 1 High-Fat Meat, 3 Fat **Carbohydrate Choices:** 4½

sweet tip

Dulce de leche, a caramelized condensed milk, can be found in the sweetened condensed milk section at the grocery store.

Tangerine Ombre Cake

PREP TIME: **1 Hour** • START TO FINISH: **2 Hours 10 Minutes** • **16 servings**

CAKE

- 1 box white cake mix with pudding
- 1¼ cups fresh tangerine or orange juice
- 1 box (4-serving size) orange-flavored gelatin
- ⅓ cup vegetable oil
- 4 eggs
  Orange gel food color

FROSTING

- 2 cups butter, softened
- 12 cups powdered sugar
- ¾ cup fresh tangerine or orange juice
- 1 tablespoon vanilla

sweet tip

If you don't have enough pans, store batter covered in the refrigerator while baking the first layers. Cool pans completely before baking the next layers.

1 Heat oven to 350°F. Grease 4 (8-inch) round cake pans with shortening or spray with cooking spray. Place 8-inch round piece of cooking parchment paper in bottom of each pan. Grease or spray paper with cooking spray.

2 In large bowl, beat all cake ingredients except food color with electric mixer on low speed 30 seconds, then on high speed about 2 minutes or until smooth. Spoon and spread 1½ cups of batter into 1 pan. Divide remaining batter evenly among 3 small bowls (about 1½ cups each). Add different amounts of food color to each to make different shades of orange. Stir each until color is well blended.

3 Pour 1 bowl of batter into each of 3 remaining pans. Baking 2 pans at a time, bake 22 to 26 minutes (refrigerate remaining pans until baking). Cool 5 minutes. Remove from pans to cooling rack; remove paper. Cool completely, about 30 minutes.

4 In large bowl, beat butter and powdered sugar with spoon or electric mixer on low speed until blended. Stir in ¾ cup tangerine juice and the vanilla. If frosting is too thick, beat in more juice, a few drops at a time. If too thin, beat in a small amount of powdered sugar.

5 To assemble, place deepest color cake layer on cake plate. Spread with ½ cup frosting. Stack layers from darkest to lightest, spreading ½ cup frosting between layers. Thinly spread top and side of cake with 1½ cups frosting to seal in crumbs.

6 Divide remaining frosting among 4 small bowls. Add different amounts of food color to each to make different shades of orange to match cake layers.

7 To frost, place each color in individual resealable food-storage plastic bag. Cut ½ inch off 1 corner of each bag; pipe each frosting on corresponding color cake layer. Pipe a dot of frosting and use

back of tablespoon to spread frosting horizontally around cake, with deepest color at bottom and working up to lighter colors. Repeat around cake slightly overlapping dots of frosting. To frost top, use remaining frosting as desired. Store cake loosely covered in refrigerator.

1 Serving: Calories 770; Total Fat 30g (Saturated Fat 16g, Trans Fat 1g); Cholesterol 110mg; Sodium 450mg; Total Carbohydrate 122g (Dietary Fiber 0g); Protein 3g **Exchanges:** 1 Starch, 7 Other Carbohydrate, 6 Fat **Carbohydrate Choices:** 8

Grasshopper Fudge Cake

PREP TIME: 20 Minutes • **START TO FINISH:** 1 Hour 55 Minutes • **15 servings**

1   box white cake mix
     with pudding

     Water, vegetable oil and
     egg whites called for on
     cake mix box

2   teaspoons mint extract

     Liquid green food color

2   jars (16 oz each) hot fudge
     topping

1   container (8 oz) frozen
     whipped topping, thawed

     Liquid yellow food color

     Thin rectangular crème de
     menthe chocolate candies,
     unwrapped, cut into pieces,
     if desired

1 Heat oven to 350°F (325°F for dark or nonstick pan). Spray bottom only of 13×9-inch pan with baking spray with flour.

2 Make cake batter as directed on box, using water, oil and eggs and adding 1½ teaspoons of the mint extract with the water. Reserve 1 cup batter. Stir 3 drops of the green food color into reserved batter; set aside. Pour remaining batter into pan.

3 Drop green batter by generous tablespoonfuls randomly in 12 to 14 mounds onto batter in pan. Cut through batters with metal spatula or knife in S-shaped curves in one continuous motion. Turn pan one-fourth turn; repeat cutting for swirled design.

4 Bake as directed on box for 13×9-inch pan. Run knife around sides of pan to loosen cake. Cool completely, about 1 hour.

5 Carefully spread fudge topping evenly over cake. In medium bowl, stir whipped topping, remaining ½ teaspoon mint extract, remaining 9 drops green food color and 5 drops yellow food color until blended. Spread whipped topping mixture evenly over fudge. Garnish with candy pieces. Store cake loosely covered in refrigerator.

1 Serving: Calories 420; Total Fat 14g (Saturated Fat 6g, Trans Fat 0g); Cholesterol 0mg; Sodium 440mg; Total Carbohydrate 67g (Dietary Fiber 2g); Protein 5g **Exchanges:** 1½ Starch, 3 Other Carbohydrate, 2½ Fat **Carbohydrate Choices:** 4½

sweet tip

Warm the foil-wrapped mints in your hands for a minute or two to make cutting them easier.

Gluten-Free
Caramel Chocolate Cake

PREP TIME: 20 Minutes • **START TO FINISH: 3 Hours** • **9 servings**

1 box Betty Crocker Gluten Free devil's food cake mix

Water, butter and eggs called for on cake mix box

1 jar (12.25 oz) caramel topping

1 cup frozen (thawed) whipped topping

½ cup toffee bits

1 Heat oven to 350°F (325°F for dark or nonstick pan).

2 Make and bake cake mix as directed on box, using water, butter, eggs and any of the pan choices.

3 With handle of wooden spoon, poke top of warm cake every ½ inch. Drizzle caramel topping evenly over top of cake; let stand until absorbed into cake. Cover; refrigerate about 2 hours or until chilled.

4 Spread whipped topping over top of cake. Sprinkle with toffee bits. Store cake loosely covered in refrigerator.

1 Serving: Calories 520; Total Fat 21g (Saturated Fat 13g, Trans Fat 0.5g); Cholesterol 115mg; Sodium 520mg; Total Carbohydrate 80g (Dietary Fiber 1g); Protein 4g **Exchanges:** 1½ Starch, 4 Other Carbohydrate, 4 Fat **Carbohydrate Choices:** 5

sweet tip

When you are cooking gluten free, always read labels to make sure each recipe ingredient is gluten free. Products and ingredient sources can change.

Lemon Champagne Celebration Cupcakes

PREP TIME: 40 Minutes • **START TO FINISH: 2 Hours 30 Minutes** • **12 cupcakes**

CUPCAKES

1	box yellow cake mix with pudding
½	cup water
½	cup dry champagne
½	cup vegetable oil
3	eggs
2	teaspoons grated lemon peel

FILLING

¼	cup lemon curd (from 10-oz jar)
1	tablespoon sour cream

ICING AND GARNISH

2	cups powdered sugar
2	tablespoons butter, melted
3	tablespoons fresh lemon juice
	Lemon peel curls, if desired

1 Heat oven to 350°F (325°F for dark or nonstick pan). Line 15×10×1-inch pan with foil; spray with cooking spray.

2 Make cake batter as directed on box, using all cake ingredients except lemon peel. Stir 2 teaspoons grated lemon peel into batter. Pour into pan.

3 Bake 17 to 23 minutes or until toothpick inserted in center comes out clean. Do not remove cake from pan. Cool completely on cooling rack, about 1 hour. Place pan of cake in freezer. Freeze 1 hour or until firm.

4 In small bowl, mix filling ingredients until well blended. Set aside.

5 To assemble cupcakes, remove cake from freezer. Using foil, lift cake from pan. With 2¼-inch round cutter, cut 24 rounds from cake. Place 12 rounds top side down. Spread each with about 1 teaspoon lemon curd filling. Top with remaining cake rounds, top side up.

6 In medium bowl, mix powdered sugar, butter and lemon juice until well blended. Spoon about 1 tablespoon icing over each cake, allowing icing to run down side of cake.

7 To serve, place each cake in decorative paper baking cup. Garnish with lemon peel curls.

1 Cupcake: Calories 270; Total Fat 11g (Saturated Fat 3g, Trans Fat 0g); Cholesterol 50mg; Sodium 220mg; Total Carbohydrate 41g (Dietary Fiber 0g); Protein 2g **Exchanges:** 1 Starch, 1½ Other Carbohydrate, 2 Fat **Carbohydrate Choices:** 3

sweet tip

You'll find lemon curd in most large supermarkets with the preserves and jellies.

Chocolate–Sour Cream Cupcakes

PREP TIME: 40 Minutes • **START TO FINISH: 1 Hour 40 Minutes** • **24 cupcakes**

CUPCAKES

2	cups all-purpose flour
⅔	cup unsweetened baking cocoa
1¼	teaspoons baking soda
1	teaspoon salt
¼	teaspoon baking powder
¾	cup shortening
1½	cups granulated sugar
2	eggs
½	cup sour cream
1	teaspoon vanilla
1	cup water

FROSTING

4	cups (1 lb) powdered sugar
1	cup butter, softened
3	to 4 tablespoons milk
1½	teaspoons vanilla
3	oz unsweetened baking chocolate, melted, cooled

1 Heat oven to 350°F. Place paper baking cup in each of 24 regular-size muffin cups.

2 In medium bowl, stir together flour, cocoa, baking soda, salt and baking powder; set aside. In large bowl, beat shortening with electric mixer on medium speed 30 seconds. Beat in granulated sugar, about ¼ cup at a time. Beat 2 minutes longer. Beat in eggs, one at a time, beating well after each addition. Beat in sour cream and vanilla until well blended. On low speed, alternately add flour mixture, about one-third at a time, and water, about half at a time, beating just until blended.

3 Divide batter evenly among muffin cups, filling each about two-thirds full.

4 Bake 20 to 25 minutes or until toothpick inserted in center of cupcake comes out clean. Cool 5 minutes. Remove from pans to cooling racks. Cool completely.

5 In medium bowl, beat frosting ingredients with electric mixer on medium speed until smooth and spreadable. If necessary, stir in additional milk, 1 teaspoon at a time. Spoon frosting into decorating bag fitted with large star tip #6. Pipe frosting onto cupcakes or frost as desired.

1 Cupcake: Calories 340; Total Fat 18g (Saturated Fat 9g, Trans Fat 1.5g); Cholesterol 40mg; Sodium 240mg; Total Carbohydrate 42g (Dietary Fiber 1g); Protein 2g **Exchanges:** 1 Starch, 2 Other Carbohydrate, 3½ Fat **Carbohydrate Choices:** 3

Gluten-Free Celebration Cupcakes

PREP TIME: 20 Minutes • **START TO FINISH: 1 Hour 10 Minutes** • **12 cupcakes**

CUPCAKES

- 1½ cups Bisquick® Gluten Free mix
- ⅔ cup milk
- ½ cup granulated sugar
- ¼ cup butter, softened
- 1 teaspoon gluten-free vanilla
- 1 egg

FROSTING

- 2½ cups powdered sugar
- ½ cup unsweetened baking cocoa
- ½ cup butter, softened
- ¼ cup milk
- 1 teaspoon gluten-free vanilla
- Candy sprinkles

1 Heat oven to 375°F. Place paper baking cup in each of 12 regular-size muffin cups.

2 In large bowl, beat cupcake ingredients with electric mixer on low speed 30 seconds, scraping bowl frequently. Beat on medium speed 2 minutes, scraping bowl occasionally. (Batter will be thick.) Divide batter evenly among muffin cups, filling each half full.

3 Bake 18 to 20 minutes or until toothpick inserted in center comes out clean. Remove from pan to cooling rack. Cool completely, about 30 minutes.

4 In small bowl, mix powdered sugar and cocoa. In large bowl, beat ½ cup butter on medium speed 2 minutes or until creamy. Add powdered sugar mixture alternately with ¼ cup milk, beating on low speed until blended. Beat in 1 teaspoon vanilla. Frost cupcakes. Garnish with candy sprinkles. Store cupcakes loosely covered in refrigerator.

1 Cupcake: Calories 330; Total Fat 13g (Saturated Fat 8g, Trans Fat 0g); Cholesterol 50mg; Sodium 290mg; Total Carbohydrate 49g (Dietary Fiber 1g); Protein 2g **Exchanges:** ½ Starch, 3 Other Carbohydrate, 2½ Fat **Carbohydrate Choices:** 3

sweet tip

When you are cooking gluten free, always read labels to make sure each recipe ingredient is gluten free. Products and ingredient sources can change.

Cinnamon Burst Cheerios Cereal Pops

PREP TIME: 35 Minutes • **START TO FINISH: 1 Hour 5 Minutes** • 36 cereal pops

1   can (14 oz) sweetened condensed milk (not evaporated)

½   cup butter

1   bag (14 oz) caramels, unwrapped

36   paper lollipop sticks

1   bag (16 oz) large marshmallows (about 36)

1   box (12 oz) Cinnamon Burst Cheerios® cereal

1 Line large cookie sheets with foil.

2 In nonstick 2-quart heavy saucepan, heat condensed milk, butter and caramels over low heat, stirring frequently, until melted and smooth. Remove from heat.

3 Insert lollipop stick into each marshmallow; dip into hot caramel. Roll in cereal to coat completely; place on cookie sheet. Refrigerate about 30 minutes or until set. Store pops in airtight container.

1 Cereal Pop: Calories 180; Total Fat 5g (Saturated Fat 2.5g, Trans Fat 0g); Cholesterol 10mg; Sodium 105mg; Total Carbohydrate 33g (Dietary Fiber 1g); Protein 2g **Exchanges:** ½ Starch, 1½ Other Carbohydrate, 1 Fat **Carbohydrate Choices:** 2

sweet tip

Unwrapping caramels is fun for kids. Make sure you have plenty of the caramels in case a few disappear.

Watermelon Pops

PREP TIME: **1 Hour** • START TO FINISH: **3 Hours 10 Minutes** • **32 cake pops**

1 box white cake mix with pudding

   Water, vegetable oil and egg whites called for on cake mix box

¼ teaspoon pink paste food color

¾ cup vanilla creamy ready-to-spread frosting (from 1-lb container)

¾ cup miniature semisweet chocolate chips

32 paper lollipop sticks

1 bag (16 oz) white candy melts or coating wafers, melted

1 block polystyrene foam

1 bag (16 oz) green candy melts or coating wafers, melted

1 cup light green candy melts or coating wafers (from 16-oz bag), melted

1 Heat oven to 350°F. Spray 13×9-inch pan with cooking spray.

2 Make and bake cake mix as directed on box for 13×9-inch pan, using water, oil and egg whites and adding food color. Cool completely.

3 Line cookie sheet with waxed paper. Crumble cake into large bowl. Add frosting and chocolate chips; mix well. Shape into 32 oblong balls; place on cookie sheet. Freeze until firm. When cake balls are firm, transfer to refrigerator.

4 To make cake pops, remove cake balls a few at a time from refrigerator. Dip tip of 1 lollipop stick ½ inch into melted white candy; insert stick no more than halfway into 1 cake ball. Dip each cake ball into melted candy to cover; tap off excess. Poke opposite end of stick into foam block. Repeat with remaining cake balls, sticks and melted candy. Let stand until set.

5 Dip each cake ball into melted green candy to cover; tap off excess. Return sticks to foam block. Let stand until set. With toothpick, decorate cake balls with light green candy to look like watermelons. Let stand until set before serving.

1 Cake Pop: Calories 310; Total Fat 15g (Saturated Fat 11g, Trans Fat 0g); Cholesterol 0mg; Sodium 160mg; Total Carbohydrate 42g (Dietary Fiber 0g); Protein 2g **Exchanges:** ½ Starch, 2½ Other Carbohydrate, 3 Fat **Carbohydrate Choices:** 3

Just Ducky
Lemonade Cake Pops

PREP TIME: 1 Hour 5 Minutes   •   **START TO FINISH:** 2 Hours 30 Minutes   •   48 cake pops

1 box lemon cake mix
with pudding

Water, vegetable oil and
eggs called for on cake
mix box

1 cup fluffy white whipped
ready-to-spread frosting
(from 12-oz container)

5 tablespoons presweetened
lemonade flavor drink mix

6 tablespoons yellow sanding
sugar

4 cups yellow candy melts
or coating wafers (24 oz)

2 tablespoons shortening

48 paper lollipop sticks

1 block polystyrene foam

96 candy eyes

96 pieces candy corn,
tips trimmed

24 orange chewy fruit-flavored
candies, unwrapped, halved

1 Make, bake and cool cake as directed on box for 13×9-inch pan, using water, oil and eggs.

2 Line cookie sheet with waxed paper. Crumble cake into large bowl. Add frosting and 3 tablespoons of the drink mix; mix well. Shape into 48 (1¼-inch) balls; place on cookie sheet. Freeze until firm. When cake balls are firm, transfer to refrigerator.

3 In small bowl, mix yellow sugar and remaining 2 tablespoons drink mix; set aside. In microwavable bowl, microwave candy melts and shortening uncovered on Medium (50%) 2 minutes, then in 15-second increments, until melted; stir until smooth.

4 To make cake pops, remove cake balls a few at a time from refrigerator. Dip tip of 1 lollipop stick about ½ inch into melted candy; insert stick no more than halfway into 1 cake ball. Return to cookie sheet. Repeat with remaining cake balls, sticks and melted candy. Refrigerate 5 minutes.

5 Remove cake pops a few at a time from refrigerator. Dip each cake ball into melted candy to cover; tap off excess. Immediately sprinkle with sugar mixture. Poke opposite end of stick into foam block. Let stand until set.

6 Use remaining melted candy to attach candy eyes, candy corn pieces for feet and orange candy for nose. Spoon melted candy on tops. Let stand until set before serving.

1 Cake Pop: Calories 190; Total Fat 9g (Saturated Fat 5g, Trans Fat 0g); Cholesterol 10mg; Sodium 100mg; Total Carbohydrate 28g (Dietary Fiber 0g); Protein 1g **Exchanges:** ½ Starch, 1½ Other Carbohydrate, 1½ Fat **Carbohydrate Choices:** 2

Dark Chocolate Fondue

PREP TIME: 25 Minutes • **START TO FINISH:** 25 Minutes • 20 servings (2½ tablespoons fondue, 1 cake piece, 2 strawberries and 2 apple slices each)

8 oz bittersweet baking chocolate, chopped

8 oz semisweet baking chocolate, chopped

1 pint (2 cups) whipping cream

1 tablespoon vanilla

1 package (10.75 oz) frozen pound cake, cut into 1-inch cubes

40 small fresh strawberries

40 apple slices

Kiwifruit, cut up, if desired

1 In 2-quart saucepan, heat both chocolates and the whipping cream over low heat, stirring frequently, until cream is hot and chocolate is melted. Stir with whisk until smooth. Stir in vanilla. Pour into fondue pot. Keep warm with fuel canister on low heat.

2 Arrange cake and fruit dippers on platter. Set fondue pot in center of platter.

1 Serving: Calories 290; Total Fat 21g (Saturated Fat 12g, Trans Fat 0.5g); Cholesterol 45mg; Sodium 25mg; Total Carbohydrate 22g (Dietary Fiber 3g); Protein 4g **Exchanges:** 1 Starch, ½ Other Carbohydrate, 4 Fat **Carbohydrate Choices:** 1½

sweet tips

Instead of the vanilla, try 1 tablespoon of orange-, cherry-, almond- or coffee-flavored liqueur.

Banana chunks, orange or tangerine segments, marshmallows or coconut macaroon cookies also make tasty dippers for this rich fondue.

Turtle Cheesecake

PREP TIME: **30 Minutes** • START TO FINISH: **4 Hours 20 Minutes** • **12 servings**

1½ cups finely crushed vanilla wafer cookies (about 40 cookies)

¼ cup butter, melted

2 packages (8 oz each) cream cheese, softened

½ cup sugar

2 teaspoons vanilla

2 eggs

¼ cup hot fudge topping

1 cup caramel topping

½ cup coarsely chopped pecans, toasted, if desired

1 Heat oven to 350°F. In medium bowl, mix cookie crumbs and butter. Press crumb mixture firmly against bottom and side of ungreased 9-inch glass pie plate.

2 In large bowl, beat cream cheese, sugar, vanilla and eggs with electric mixer on low speed until smooth. Pour half of mixture into pie plate.

3 Add hot fudge topping to remaining cream cheese mixture in bowl; beat on low speed until smooth. Spoon over vanilla mixture in pie plate. Swirl mixtures slightly with tip of knife.

4 Bake 40 to 50 minutes or until center is set. Cool 1 hour. Refrigerate at least 2 hours until chilled. Serve with caramel topping and pecans. Store cheesecake covered in refrigerator.

1 Serving: Calories 390; Total Fat 24g (Saturated Fat 12g, Trans Fat 1g); Cholesterol 85mg; Sodium 310mg; Total Carbohydrate 39g (Dietary Fiber 1g); Protein 6g **Exchanges:** 1½ Starch, 1 Other Carbohydrate, 4½ Fat **Carbohydrate Choices:** 2½

Healthified Mini Chocolate Cheesecakes

PREP TIME: 20 Minutes • **START TO FINISH: 2 Hours 25 Minutes** • **12 servings**

CHEESECAKES

- 12 foil baking cups
- 12 thin chocolate wafer cookies (from 9-oz package), crushed (⅔ cup)
- 12 oz ⅓-less-fat cream cheese (Neufchâtel), softened
- ⅔ cup sugar
- 2 teaspoons vanilla
- ¼ cup unsweetened baking cocoa
- 1 whole egg
- 1 egg white
- 1 oz bittersweet or semisweet baking chocolate, melted

TOPPING

- ⅓ cup fat-free hot fudge topping
- Fresh raspberries, if desired

1 Heat oven to 325°F. Place foil baking cup in each of 12 regular-size muffin cups.

2 With back of spoon, firmly press slightly less than 1 tablespoon cookie crumbs in bottom of each foil cup.

3 In large bowl, beat cream cheese with electric mixer on medium speed until creamy. Beat in sugar and vanilla until fluffy. Beat in cocoa. Beat in whole egg and egg white until well blended. Stir in melted chocolate. Divide cheese mixture evenly among crumb-lined foil cups.

4 Bake 28 to 32 minutes or until set. Cool in pan on cooling rack 15 minutes. Remove cheesecakes from pan; cool 15 minutes longer. Refrigerate about 1 hour or until chilled.

5 To serve, carefully remove foil baking cups. Spread fudge topping on cheesecakes. Garnish with raspberries. Store cheesecakes covered in refrigerator.

1 Serving: Calories 200; Total Fat 9g (Saturated Fat 5g, Trans Fat 0g); Cholesterol 40mg; Sodium 180mg; Total Carbohydrate 25g (Dietary Fiber 1g); Protein 4g **Exchanges:** 1 Starch, ½ Other Carbohydrate, 2 Fat **Carbohydrate Choices:** 1½

sweet tips

We recommend using ⅓-less-fat cream cheese. When testing the recipe with fat-free cream cheese, we found the cheesecakes to have poor texture and a bland flavor. If you choose to try fat-free cream cheese, we suggest using 4 ounces fat-free cream cheese and 8 ounces ⅓-less-fat cream cheese.

If fudge topping is too thick to spread, place in small microwavable bowl and microwave uncovered on High 15 to 30 seconds or until spreadable. Stir before spreading.

Chocolate-Cherry
Ice Cream Cake

PREP TIME: 25 Minutes • **START TO FINISH:** 9 Hours 45 Minutes • **12 servings**

16   creme-filled chocolate
       sandwich cookies

¼   cup butter

1   quart (4 cups) cherry or
       cherry vanilla ice cream,
       softened

8   creme-filled chocolate
       sandwich cookies, coarsely
       chopped

1   cup miniature semisweet
       chocolate chips

1   quart (4 cups) vanilla
       ice cream, softened

½   cup fudge topping

       Sweetened whipped cream,
       if desired

12   fresh cherries with stems

1 Heat oven to 350°F. Place 16 cookies in food processor. Cover; process until finely ground. Add butter; cover and process until mixed. Press in ungreased 9-inch springform pan. Bake 8 to 10 minutes or until firm. Cool completely, about 30 minutes.

2 Wrap outside of springform pan with foil. Spread cherry ice cream over cooled crust. Freeze 30 minutes.

3 Sprinkle chopped cookies and ½ cup of the chocolate chips over cherry ice cream; press slightly. Spread vanilla ice cream over top. Drop fudge topping over ice cream in small spoonfuls; swirl slightly into ice cream. Sprinkle with remaining ½ cup chocolate chips; press slightly. Freeze about 8 hours or until firm.

4 To serve, let stand at room temperature 5 to 10 minutes. Carefully remove side of pan. Cut into wedges. Top each wedge with whipped cream and cherry.

1 Serving: Calories 460; Total Fat 24g (Saturated Fat 13g, Trans Fat 0.5g); Cholesterol 50mg; Sodium 240mg; Total Carbohydrate 57g (Dietary Fiber 2g); Protein 5g **Exchanges:** 1½ Starch, 2 Other Carbohydrate, 4½ Fat **Carbohydrate Choices:** 4

sweet tips

Spray the back of a metal spoon with cooking spray, then use it to press the crumb mixture into the pan.

It's a snap to spread the fudge topping over the ice cream. Just spoon the topping into a resealable food-storage plastic bag, cut off a small tip from one corner and squeeze.

Cheesecake Shot-Glass Desserts

PREP TIME: 30 Minutes • **START TO FINISH:** 1 Hour • **12 servings**

2 packages (8 oz each) cream cheese, softened

¾ cup sugar

1 tablespoon coffee-flavored liqueur or 1 teaspoon chocolate extract

2 teaspoons grated lemon peel

4 tablespoons chocolate cookie crumbs

Chocolate-covered coffee beans or grated chocolate

4 tablespoons graham cracker crumbs

Blueberries and raspberries

1 In large bowl, beat cream cheese and sugar with electric mixer on medium speed until smooth. Divide mixture in half; place in separate bowls. Stir coffee liqueur into half of cream cheese mixture; stir lemon peel into remaining half.

2 Spoon 2 teaspoons chocolate cookie crumbs into bottom of each of 6 (2-oz) cordial glasses (shot glasses). Top each with 2 tablespoons coffee liqueur–cream cheese mixture. Sprinkle with 2 teaspoons cookie crumbs. Add another 2 tablespoons coffee liqueur–cream cheese mixture. Top each with coffee bean.

3 Spoon 2 teaspoons graham cracker crumbs into bottom of each of 6 (2-oz) cordial glasses (shot glasses). Top each with 2 tablespoons lemon–cream cheese mixture. Sprinkle with 2 teaspoons graham cracker crumbs. Add another 2 tablespoons lemon–cream cheese mixture. Top each with blueberries and raspberries. Refrigerate at least 30 minutes before serving.

1 Serving: Calories 210; Total Fat 14g (Saturated Fat 9g, Trans Fat 0.5g); Cholesterol 40mg; Sodium 135mg; Total Carbohydrate 19g (Dietary Fiber 0g); Protein 3g **Exchanges:** 1 Other Carbohydrate, ½ High-Fat Meat, 2 Fat **Carbohydrate Choices:** 1

sweet tip

This is a great opportunity to use any souvenir shot glasses you have on hand. Or use 2-ounce plastic cups available in party supply stores.

Lemon-Ginger Icebox Cookie Cupcakes

PREP TIME: **1 Hour 10 Minutes** • START TO FINISH: **12 Hours 40 Minutes** • **16 cookie cupcakes**

COOKIES

- 1   pouch (1 lb 1.5 oz) sugar cookie mix
- ½   cup butter, softened
- 1   egg
- 1   tablespoon grated lemon peel
- ⅓   cup finely chopped crystallized ginger

FILLING

- 2   cups whipping cream
- ¼   cup powdered sugar
- 1   teaspoon vanilla

1 In medium bowl, stir cookie mix, butter, egg and lemon peel until soft dough forms. Stir in crystallized ginger. Divide dough in half. On waxed paper, shape each half into 8-inch-long roll. Wrap in waxed paper. Freeze about 1 hour or refrigerate about 3 hours until firm enough to slice.

2 Heat oven to 350°F. Using a sharp thin-bladed knife, cut each roll into 32 (⅛-inch-thick) slices. Rotate roll while cutting to prevent flattening. On ungreased cookie sheets, place slices 1 inch apart.

3 Bake 9 to 11 minutes, or until edges are light brown. Cool 1 minute. Remove from cookie sheets to cooling rack. Cool completely, about 30 minutes.

4 In chilled small deep bowl, beat filling ingredients with electric mixer on high speed until stiff peaks form. On tray, place 16 cookies right sides up. Spread 1 tablespoon whipped cream on top of each cookie, then top with another cookie. Repeat with remaining cookies and cream, making 4 layers of cookies and ending with a layer of cream. Place each cookie cupcake in a decorative paper baking cup. Cover with plastic wrap; refrigerate at least 8 hours. If desired, garnish with raspberries, strawberries and blueberries.

1 Cookie Cupcake: Calories 290; Total Fat 18g (Saturated Fat 10g, Trans Fat 1.5g); Cholesterol 60mg; Sodium 140mg; Total Carbohydrate 30g (Dietary Fiber 0g); Protein 2g **Exchanges:** 1 Starch, 1 Other Carbohydrate, 3½ Fat **Carbohydrate Choices:** 2

sweet tip

Refrigerate at least 8 hours before serving to allow the cookies to soften to desired cakelike texture. The cookie cupcakes can be stored in the refrigerator for up to 24 hours before serving.

Metric Conversion Guide

Volume

U.S. UNITS	CANADIAN METRIC	AUSTRALIAN METRIC
¼ teaspoon	1 mL	1 ml
½ teaspoon	2 mL	2 ml
1 teaspoon	5 mL	5 ml
1 tablespoon	15 mL	20 ml
¼ cup	50 mL	60 ml
⅓ cup	75 mL	80 ml
½ cup	125 mL	125 ml
⅔ cup	150 mL	170 ml
¾ cup	175 mL	190 ml
1 cup	250 mL	250 ml
1 quart	1 liter	1 liter
1½ quarts	1.5 liters	1.5 liters
2 quarts	2 liters	2 liters
2½ quarts	2.5 liters	2.5 liters
3 quarts	3 liters	3 liters
4 quarts	4 liters	4 liters

Weight

U.S. UNITS	CANADIAN METRIC	AUSTRALIAN METRIC
1 ounce	30 grams	30 grams
2 ounces	55 grams	60 grams
3 ounces	85 grams	90 grams
4 ounces (¼ pound)	115 grams	125 grams
8 ounces (½ pound)	225 grams	225 grams
16 ounces (1 pound)	455 grams	500 grams
1 pound	455 grams	0.5 kilogram

Note: The recipes in this cookbook have not been developed or tested using metric measures. When converting recipes to metric, some variations in quality may be noted.

Measurements

INCHES	CENTIMETERS
1	2.5
2	5.0
3	7.5
4	10.0
5	12.5
6	15.0
7	17.5
8	20.5
9	23.0
10	25.5
11	28.0
12	30.5
13	33.0

Temperatures

FAHRENHEIT	CELSIUS
32°	0°
212°	100°
250°	120°
275°	140°
300°	150°
325°	160°
350°	180°
375°	190°
400°	200°
425°	220°
450°	230°
475°	240°
500°	260°

Index

Page numbers in *italics* indicate illustrations

Recipe Testing and Calculating Nutrition Information

RECIPE TESTING:

- Large eggs and 2% milk were used unless otherwise indicated.
- Fat-free, low-fat, low-sodium or lite products were not used unless indicated.
- No nonstick cookware and bakeware were used unless otherwise indicated. No dark-colored, black or insulated bakeware was used.
- When a pan is specified, a metal pan was used; a baking dish or pie plate means ovenproof glass was used.
- An electric hand mixer was used for mixing only when mixer speeds are specified.

CALCULATING NUTRITION:

- The first ingredient was used wherever a choice is given, such as ⅓ cup sour cream or plain yogurt.
- The first amount was used wherever a range is given, such as 3- to 3½-pound whole chicken.
- The first serving number was used wherever a range is given, such as 4 to 6 servings.
- "If desired" ingredients were not included.
- Only the amount of a marinade or frying oil that is absorbed was included.